Greatest Scientists of the World

Published by:

F-2/16, Ansari road, Daryaganj, New Delhi-110002
☎ 23240026, 23240027 • *Fax:* 011-23240028
✉ info@vspublishers.com • 🌐 www.vspublishers.com

Online Brandstore: amazon.in/vspublishers

Regional Office : Hyderabad
5-1-707/1, Brij Bhawan (Beside Central Bank of India Lane)
Bank Street, Koti, Hyderabad - 500 095
☎ 040-24737290
✉ vspublishershyd@gmail.com

Follow us on:

BUY OUR BOOKS FROM: AMAZON FLIPKART

ISBN 978-93-505717-5-0
New Edition

Printed at : Param Offsetters, Okhla, New Delhi–110020

Publisher's Note

It's truely said by Stephen Hawking that *Scientists have become the bearers of the torch of discovery in our quest for knowledge.*

We are glad to inform all our esteemed readers that V&S Publishers is coming out with a number of books in the ***Greatest Series*** which include *Classic Storybooks of great authors* like *Sir Arthur Conan Doyle,* (the creator of the famous fictional character, Sherlock Holmes), Charles Dickens, Ambrose Bierce, Jack London, O. Henry and others. This book on ***Scientists*** is an addition in the Greatest Series.

The book contains information about *101 world-renowned Scientists* from *across the globe,* their brief life sketch, their contributions to the scientific world including books, journals and magazines that they published, Awards and Honours received by them and any significant incidents that changed the course of their lives. The book includes prominent names like, *Sir Isaac Newton, Ivan Pavlov, J.J Thomson, Jagadish Chandra Bose, James Clerk Maxwell, James Watson, Jean-Baptiste Lamarck, John Dalton, John Logie Baird, Louis Pasteur* and many such notable personalities.

The book has been written especially for the *school students of the age group, 10-18 years,* but it can be read by readers of all ages, who love Science and its amazing and fascinating world full of outstanding inventions and discoveries that have almost changed or rather transformed the human society and even our existence.

So, the book will be of interest for one and all, especially for students, who can use it as a valuable reference book too!

Contents

Isaac Newton

Sir Isaac Newton, universally considered to be one of the greatest and most influential scientists of all time, was an English mathematician and physicist, widely known for his outstanding contributions to physics, mathematics and optics. He also invented the calculus, formulated the three laws of motion and the universal theory of gravitation. Newton proved that sunlight is the combination of several colours. He performed as the *master of the Royal Mint in London* and as the *president of the Royal Society of London.*

Born on January 4, 1643, Newton was so frail at the time of his birth that the housemaids were unsure that the baby would live any longer. Isaac Sr. had died a few months before his birth, while his mother, Hannah Ayscough, married again to another man, Reverend Barnabas Smith, with whom she had three more children.

His mother left little Newton to live with her new husband, while he was raised by his maternal grandmother. Newton had mostly a solitary childhood, though at 12, he joined the grammar school at Grantham. At school, once he had a fight with another boy, and whilst he was weaker, he still managed to win the fight and banged the opponent's nose on the church wall. This kind of vindictive behaviour endured throughout his lifetime.

Creating sundials, wooden objects and drawings were some of his *favourite hobbies at school.* He made a model windmill with a mouse on a treadmill for supplying power. A four-wheeled cart was also one of his creations which was powered by rotating a crank he had set up.

His mother called Newton back to manage the family farm when he was 17. He was never good at the job, though. *A young Newton showed more interest in creating models and reading books.* Luckily enough, his schoolmaster at Grantham, and his uncle William Ayscough, utterly impressed with Newton's skill and determination, suggested his mother to let him stay at the school.

After finishing school in June 1661, Newton went on to join the Cambridge University. There, he was annoyed with the traditional Aristotelian curriculum and shunned many of the assigned books, instead concentrating on his studies about science, mathematics and philosophy. He carefully and devotedly read books by *Galileo, René Descartes, Euclid and Johannes Kepler.* Within a year, he was able to record original insights in his notebooks.

Not long after his graduation in 1665, the Cambridge closed down due to the plague epidemic for almost two years. Newton, therefore, returned to home where he came up with the calculus, which he termed as the "fluxional method." Isaac Barrow, the Lucasian professor of Mathematics at Cambridge, was immensely impressed with his work. Newton got his master's degree in 1668, and assumed Barrow's position after his resignation. His lectures were said to be too difficult for the students.

Contributions & Achievements:

His contributions during 1669 and the early 1770s were mostly *related to optics.* He put forward a theory of colours. He also constructed a reflecting telescope which magnified objects 40 times. For this invention, he was honoured by The Royal Society, where he was made a member in January 1672. An article was published during this time about his theory of colours in February 1672. When Robert Hooke challenged him in an inappropriate manner, Newton was furious. He had experimented with colours extensively for several years and was confident about his peculiar ability and research.

Newton published his legendary publication, "Philosophiae Naturalis Principia Mathematica" in 1687, a masterpiece that introduced the world to the *three laws of motion* and the *universal principle of gravitation.*

His another notable rival was *Gottfried Wilhelm Leibniz* who claimed to have invented the calculus first. As *Newton's Principia* came after *Leibniz's calculus,* some started to think that Newton borrowed his method from Leibniz. The truth was that Newton had invented the calculus between 1665 and 1666, but he was reluctant to publish his work for years, while Leibniz introduced his work in 1684. Leibniz actually received letters from Newton in 1671 and 1676 regarding mathematics, and he was either directly or indirectly influenced by Newton. The feud settled down in 1716 after Leibniz's death.

Newton is also credited with the generalised binomial theorem, valid for any exponent. Newton soon got bored with academia, so he became the warden of the Royal Mint in 1696. He revolutionized its operations and was made a master of the Mint in 1700. He was also selected as the president of the Royal Society from 1703 until his death. Queen Anne knighted Newton in 1705. In his final years, Newton suffered from several physical illnesses. He died on March 20, 1727 in London, England.

Ivan Pavlov

1849 – 1936

Ivan Petrovich Pavlov was an eminent Russian physiologist and psychologist who devised the concept of the conditioned reflex. He conducted a legendary experiment in which he provided training to a hungry dog to drool at the sound of a bell, something which was related to the sight of food.

Pavlov also formulated a similar conceptual theory, highlighting the significance of conditioning and associating human behaviour with the nervous system. He won the *1904 Nobel Prize for Physiology* or *Medicine* for his groundbreaking *research on digestive secretions.*

Ivan Pavlov was born in *Ryazan, Russia.* As a young child, he suffered a serious injury, due to which Pavlov spent much of his childhood with his parents in the family home and garden, acquiring various practical skills and a deep interest in natural history. He developed a strong interest in science and the possibility of using science to ameliorate and modify society.

He studied medicine at the university under a famed *physiologist of the time, S. P. Botkin,* who taught him a great deal about the nervous system.

Contributions & Achievements:

Ivan Pavlov conducted neurophysiological experiments with animals for years after receiving his doctorate at the Academy of Medical Surgery. He became fully convinced that human behaviour could be understood and explained best in physiological terms rather than in mentalist terms. The legendary experiment for which Pavlov is remembered was when he used the feeding of dogs to establish a number of his key ideas.

Moments before feeding, a bell was rung to measure the dogs' saliva production when they heard the bell. Pavolv found out that once the dogs had been trained to associate the sound of the bell with food, they would produce saliva, whether or not food followed. The experiment proved that the dogs' physical response and salivation was directly related to the stimulus of the bell, and hence, the saliva production was a stimulus response. The continued increased salivation, even when the dogs had experienced hearing the bell without being later fed, was a *conditioned reflex.*

The entire process is a prime example of classical conditioning, and it is primarily related to a physical and spontaneous response to some particular conditions that the organism has acquired through association. *The Behaviourist Theory* has massively applied these landmark ideas for the explanation of human behaviour.

Ivan Pavlov died on February 27, 1936 in Leningrad, Soviet Union, from natural causes. He was 86 years old.

J. J. Thomson

Sir Joseph John Thomson, more commonly known as *J. J. Thomson*, was an English physicist who stormed the world of nuclear physics with his 1897 discovery of the *electron,* as well as *isotopes*. He is also credited with the invention of the *mass spectrometer.* He received the *Nobel Prize for Physics in 1906* and was *knighted two years later in 1908.*

Born in 1856 in Cheetham Hill near Manchester, England, J. J. Thomson was the son of a Scottish bookseller. He won a scholarship to Trinity College, Cambridge in 1876. He received his BA in 1880 in mathematics, and MA in 1883.

J. J. Thomson was appointed a *Fellow of the Royal Society in* 1865. He was a successor to Lord Rayleigh as Cavendish Professor of Experimental Physics. His favourite student *Ernst Rutherford* later succeeded him in 1919. The early theoretical work of Thomson broadened the electromagnetic theories of James Clerk Maxwell's, which revolutionised the study of gaseous conductors of electricity, as well as the nature of cathode rays.

Contributions & Achievements:

Inspired by Wilhelm Röntgen's 1895 discovery of X-rays, Thomson demonstrated that cathode rays were actually some speedily moving particles. After measuring their speed and specific charge, he concluded that these *'corpuscles' (electrons)* were about 2000 times smaller in mass as compared to the *hydrogen ion, the lightest-known atomic particle.* The discovery, made public during Thomson's 1897 lecture to the Royal Institution, was labelled as the most influential breakthrough in the history of physics since Sir Isaac Newton.

Thomson also researched on the nature of positive rays in 1911, which significantly helped in the discovery of *Isotopes*. He proved that isotopes could be broken by deflecting positive rays in electric and magnetic fields, which was later named *mass spectrometry.*

J. J. Thomson was awarded the *Nobel Prize for physics in 1906.* He *was knighted in 1908.* He published his autobiography "Recollections and Reflections" in 1936. Thomson is widely considered to be one of the greatest scientists ever, and the most influential pioneer of Nuclear Physics.

J. J. Thomson was made the *Master of Trinity College, Cambridge in 1918,* where he remained until his death. He died on August 30, 1940. He was 83 years old. Thomson was buried close to Isaac Newton in Westminster Abbey.

J. Robert Oppenheimer

1904 – 1967

J. Robert Oppenheimer, also known as 'the *father of the atomic bomb'*, was an American nuclear physicist and director of the *Los Alamos Laboratory* (Manhattan Project). With a project so big that involved the hard work of hundreds of gifted scientists, it may appear quite undue to give so much credit on the shoulders of Oppenheimer. O*ppenheimer is, however, still the sole creator and inventor of the nuclear bomb to most people in the world.*

Born in 1904 in New York City to a rich Jewish father, Oppenheimer became one of the brightest students at the Harvard University at a youthful age of seventeen. He also went to Cambridge University in England for higher studies, where Ernest Rutherford, the famous British chemist and physicist, was his teacher. Oppenheimer acquired his Ph.D. from the University of Göttingen in Germany.

Contributions & Achievements:

Although he spent most of his time carrying out research and publishing books about the *quantum theory* and *theoretical physics,* he was probably more interested in the Classics and Eastern philosophy. In 1929, Oppenheimer topped in all the units at the University of California and the California Institute of Technology. Most of the times, Oppenheimer had almost no time for his personal life. The growing popularity of Nazism in Germany during the 1930s, however, became a major event in his life, as it led him towards politics and resistance against the European fascist movement.

Oppenheimer subsequently joined left-wing politics and became associated with several left-leaning organizations, which were somehow linked to the Communist Party.

Niels Bohr and other European scientists informed their American contemporaries about the Kaiser Wilhelm Institute's successful attempt of *splitting the atom in 1939.* President Roosevelt was much concerned that the Nazis may utilise this extraordinary technology to create an atomic weapon. This fear led him to institute the *Manhattan Project in 1941.*

Oppenheimer was appointed the scientific director of the project. He advised that the project be housed at Los Alamos in New Mexico. After extensive hard work and rigorous struggle, the first nuclear bomb was exploded on July 16, 1945, with the power of approximately 18,000 tons of TNT, at Alamogordo Air Force Base in southern New Mexico.

Within one month, two atomic bombs were dropped on Japan. The event almost instantly ended the war, after which *Oppenheimer was made the chairperson of the U.S. Atomic Energy Commission.*

Oppenheimer, due to his conscience and regrets over making such horrible weapons of mass destruction, opposed the development of the hydrogen bomb in 1949. The bomb is often thought to be the Truman administration's answer to the Soviet acquisition of the atomic bomb. Due to this unexpected move, Edward Teller, his colleague at Los Alamos, was made the director of the new project. Oppenheimer's patriotism was also questioned and he was even accused of "communist sympathies" due to his past political affiliations.

For the rest of his life, he shunned politics and performed his duties as the director of the Institute of Advanced Study at Princeton. Oppenheimer died of cancer in Princeton in 1967.

Jagadish Chandra Bose

1858 – 1937

Sir Jagadish Chandra Bose is one of the most prominent first Indian scientists who proved by experimentation that both animals and plants share much in common. He demonstrated that plants are also sensitive to heat, cold, light, noise and various other external stimuli. Bose contrived a very sophisticated instrument called *Crescograph* which could record and observe the *minute responses* because of *external stimulants.* It was capable of magnifying the motion of plant tissues to about 10,000 times of their actual size, which found many similarities between *plants and other living organisms.*

Contributions & Achievements:

The central hall of the Royal Society in London was jam-packed with famous scientists on May 10, 1901. Everyone seemed to be curious to know how Bose's experiment will demonstrate that plants have feelings like other living beings and humans. Bose chose a plant whose mots were cautiously dipped up to its stem in a vessel holding the bromide solution. *The salts of hydrobromic acid are considered a poison.* He plugged in the instrument with the plant and viewed the lighted spot on a screen showing the *movements of the plant, as its pulse beat,* and the spot began to and fro movement similar to a pendulum. Within minutes, the spot vibrated in a violent manner and finally came to an abrupt stop. The whole thing was almost like a poisoned rat fighting against death. The plant had died due to the exposure to the poisonous bromide solution.

The event was greeted with much appreciation, however some physiologists were not content, and considered Bose as an intruder. They harshly knocked the experiment but Bose did not give up and was quite confident about his findings.

Using the Crescograph, he further *researched the response of the plants to fertilizers, light rays and wireless waves.* The instrument received widespread acclaim, particularly from the P*ath Congress of Science in 1900.* Many physiologists also supported his findings later on, using more advanced instruments.

Jagadish Chandra Bose was born on November 30, 1858 at Mymensingh, now in Bangladesh. He was raised in a home committed to pure Indian traditions and culture. He got his elementary education from a vernacular school, because his father thought that Bose should learn his own mother tongue, Bengali, before studying a foreign language like English. *Bose attended Cambridge after studying physics at the Calcutta University.* He returned to India in 1884 after completing a B.Sc. degree from the Cambridge University.

Bose authored two illustrious books; '*Response in the Living and Non-living* (1902) and *'The Nervous Mechanism of Plants* (1926). He also extensively researched the behaviour of radiowaves. Mostly known as a plant physiologist, he was actually a physicist. Bose devised another instrument called *'Coherer', for detecting the radiowaves.*

Prior to his death in 1937, Bose set up the *Bose Institute at Calcutta.* He was elected the *Fellow of the Royal Society* in 1920 for his amazing contributions and Achievementss.

James Chadwick

James Chadwick was an English man and a *Physicist by profession.* He was born on October 20, 1891 in Manchester. His parents Anne Mary Knowles Chadwick and John Joseph had him as their eldest son. Chadwick got admitted in the Victoria University, Manchester. He was more interested in studying mathematics but instead he was admitted in the field of physics mistakenly. Chadwick was pretty bashful as a person so he did not make any attempt to amend the error. In 1911, he passed out of the *Honours School of Physics as a Graduate*. He further continued his studies at the same school in the laboratory of Ernest Rutherford.

Contributions & Achievements:

Rutherford gave his *atom's planetary theory* at the same place. Chadwick was acquainted to *Niels Bohr and Hans Geiger* at the department of Physics. In 1913, a degree of Master's was received by Chadwick after which he was honoured with the *Exhibition Scholarship of 1851*. He used that scholarship to finance his education at Physikalisch-Technische Reichsanstalt which was the first institution of research in Germany in Charlottenburg near Berlin. The institute worked under Geiger. One of his early works included the development of beta particles' energy range. This gave helped Wolfgang Pauli to suggest the existence of neutrino.

Chadwick served many years in a civilian camp in World War I in Ruhleben. His fellowship was used by him at Caius College and Gonville after he returned to England to work at the Cavendish Laboratory at the University of Cambridge with Rutherford. He was the pioneer at using the direct method to determine the nucleus's electric charge. He gained a position as *Research director in* 1922 as Rutherford's subordinate.

They spent a lot of time together experimenting of element alteration and also attempted to split up the nucleus of a certain element to form other elements.

There was a certain irregularity faced by both of them and they found out that every element had *an atomic mass* and *an atomic number.* And in all cases, the atomic *masses were more than the atomic numbers.* Rutherford said this might be due to the existence of proton mass particles but with impartial charge. But they were unable to find any such particle. Later, Chadwick found out in Joliot-Curies' work that after beryllium is kept open to alpha particles, it becomes radioactive. Chadwick showed in an experiment that when a nitrogen particle is exposed to radiations then it makes them recoil with a large amount of energy and that such things could happen only by the collision of particles that are uncharged and have the approximate protons' mass. In 1935, he received a *Nobel Prize* by proving that the neutrons existed.

Chadwick held Lyon Jones's position at the Liverpool University from the year, 1935 to 1948. Then from 1943 to 1946, he provided services to the *British Mission* as the *Head of Project of Manhattan.* He was also present at the first atomic test in the desert of New Mexico.

In 1945, *he got knighted and also got elected as the Caius and Gonville College Master in 1948.* He retired from this position somewhere in 1959. It was after three years that he retired from his post at the *Atomic Energy Authority of United Kingdom,* where he had worked since 1957. He passed away on July 24, 1974 in Cambridge.

James Clerk Maxwell

1831-1879

James Clerk Maxwell was born on June 13, 1831 in Edinburgh, Scotland. He was a *physicist by profession* and gave out very important theories on *electromagnetism.* He has been very intelligent as a child. From the very beginning, he solved many *complex problems of geometry.* It was due to both Maxwell's heredity and surroundings that he was a genius and observed things, and both these factors influenced his life very strongly.

Maxwell's family was also well known for their extraordinary accomplishments. He spent his childhood living with his family and other relatives in a country house, where the weather was warm and healthy. His mother passed away when he was young and as a result he grew more closer to his father. Maxwell was never one of the achievers.

It was said that he had strange ways and it was majorly due to his bashfulness and his country ways. But along with his shyness came many other traits like he had an amazing imagination and almost made any experiment possible that everyone thought was impossible. He also had the *art of public speaking* and explained *extremely complex things to people in a very simple way.*

James Clerk Maxwell belonged to the families of Maxwell and Clerk. A house in Edinburgh and countryside land was inherited by his father. Maxwell was born before their house was built and soon after they were born, his parents moved. Maxwell's father was a lawyer by profession.

Maxwell was interested in science and also in making mechanical tools and devices. Maxwell, at a very young age, was involved in everything his father did. He had a different way of learning things and no one could teach him the way he learnt. This problem was faced by him after his mother died.

After many problems, he was admitted in the *Edinburgh Academy* by his aunt and father. His first year at school was very difficult. His fellows at school gave him a hard time and mocked him for the way he dressed up or spoke. They even gave him a nickname, 'Drafty'. But later on, he proved to be a very intelligent boy and his fellows cooled down a bit.

Maxwell was highly interested in geometry and at a very young age of fifteen, he wrote his findings about ovals and double foci ellipses. His father presented the findings to a Professor named Forbes who taught at *the Edinburgh Royal Society.*

Although many things presented by Maxwell were already there but still the Professor was amazed that all these findings came from such a young boy who had very less experience of studies.

At the age of 16, he joined a university at Edinburgh in 1847. He wrote two more papers and gave them out at the *Edinburgh Royal Society.* After graduating from Edinburgh, his father got him admitted at Peterhouse but soon after that he got himself transferred because he thought he, could get a fellowship there.

He went to Trinity from 1851 to 1854. After graduation, he was offered a fellowship. Then he went to the Marischal College so that he could be close to his father who was unwell. But his father passed away soon and then he took a position in 1855 at Marischal.

He married Katherine Dewar in 1858.

After leaving Marischal due to a merger, he started working in London at the King's College. He did some remarkable work there and later he resigned in 1865. After that, he spent most of his time working on his book at his country house.

To stay in touch in academics, he did some consulting and checking work for the *University of Cambridge.* It was his efforts that laid the foundation for the development of the *Cavendish Laboratory* as he encouraged them to teach *heat and electromagnetism* courses. He was the first professor at the Cavendish Laboratory.

He spent eight years over there and worked on the experiment papers of Henry Cavendish. In 1879, Maxwell started becoming ill and he could barely walk after he returned to Cambridge. Maxwell finally passed away in Cambridge on November 5, 1879 due to abdominal cancer.

Maxwell further worked on the work of James Prescott Joule and introduced his *kinetic theory and electromagnetic fields' theory.* It was recognised by both the researchers that heat wasn't a fluid like it was once thought to be and gas molecules' velocity was measured by both of them.

Maxwell gave a new light of understanding to the theories. Joules demonstrated only the communities of science that could be measured or proven, while Maxwell went ahead with *models of mathematics* that left no queries behind and no questions unanswered.

He also took help of statistics to explain the high possibility of how the projected laws would express the matter's behaviour. Due to this law determinism was taken away looking at the possibility of this law. This is what showed a new *light to modern physics.* It was only due to this law that the Relativity Theory of Einstein was developed.

Maxwell experimented to calculate the exact velocity of the molecules of a gas and found out the faster the molecules move, more the heat was generated which meant that the movement and heat created were directly proportional to each other.

The experiment showed heat as unquestionably as a movement of particle property and not as a liquid moving from one thing to another. It was also proved that heat could control the particles' movement.

Maxwell explained a query of *Faraday's magnetic and electric field's theory* with some extremely complicated mathematical calculations that even Faraday could not explain himself.

It was explained by him that there was a force field that surrounded particles that were charged. A *mathematical mode* -1 was created by him through which he showed that the magnetic *fields* and electric fields worked together. This is why he introduced the term 'Electromagnetic'.

This was a very essential discovery in the field of chemistry as later on it helped in the *invention of an electron.* The electron was discovered by *Joseph John Thomson* when he was carrying out an experiment on an electromagnetic field to find out its effects on gases by using the principle of Maxwell. Also, investigations on light's effects on elements were based on the works of Maxwell.

It was Maxwell's work on the *velocity of vacillation of fields of electromagnetism* which said that light was to be considered as a radiation of electromagnetic form. This had quite a different impact on the theories of light.

Maxwell was a man of capabilities out of this world. His inventions in the field of heat and light can prove his capabilities. He was not a distant person and he highly appreciated others who had extraordinary capabilities and could not ignore them.

Josiah Willard Gibbs was a man who was not getting attention that he deserved, so Maxwell created a model based on *Gibbs' work* that was *three dimensional* and named it after Gibbs. This work was done by him in his dying days.

James Prescott Joule

1784 – 1858

James Prescott Joule was an English physicist who studied the nature of heat and established its relationship with mechanical work. He, therefore, laid the foundation for the *theory of conservation of energy,* which later influenced the *First Law of Thermodynamics.* He also formulated the *Joule's laws* which deal with the *transfer of energy.*

Born in Salford, Lancashire on December 24, 1818, James Prescott Joule's father was a rich brewer. Joule was mostly homeschooled. He studied arithmetic and geometry under John Dalton at the 'Manchester Literary and Philosophical Society'. He was later taught by famous scientist and lecturer, John Davies.

Contributions & Achievements:

James Prescott Joule analysed the nature of heat, and established its relationship to mechanical energy. His efforts had a profound influence on the *theory of conversation of energy (the First Law of Thermodynamics).* He collaborated with Lord Kelvin on the formulation of the absolute scale of temperature, and carried out an extensive research on *magnetostriction; a property of ferromagnetic materials that makes them modify their shapes when exposed to a magnetic field.*

Joule was the first scientist to identify this property in 1842 during an experiment with a sample of nickel. He established the relationship between the flow of current through a resistance and the heat dissipated, which was later termed as the *Joule's Law.* He is also credited with the first-ever calculation of the velocity of a gas molecule. The derived unit of *energy or work,* the *Joule*, is named after him.

Joule was elected to the *Royal Society of London* and was given a *Copley Award.* He also served as the *president of the British Association for the Advancement of Science.*

James Prescott Joule died on October 11, 1889 in Sale, Greater Manchester, England. He was 70 years old.

James Watson

Born 1928

James Dewey Watson was an *American geneticist and biophysicist.* Noted for his decisive works in the discovery of the *molecular structure of DNA*, the hereditary material associated with the transmission of genetic information. He shared the *Nobel Prize for Physiology or Medicine with Francis Crick* and *Maurice Wilkins in 1962.*

James Watson was born in 1928 in Chicago, Illinois and his father was a tax collector of the Scottish ancestry. He attended the University of Chicago, Indiana University and the Cavendish Laboratory of the University of Cambridge with Francis Crick. He was appointed a faculty member at the Harvard University, and a few years later, the director of the Cold Spring Harbour Laboratory.

James Watson gained worldwide fame and prominence as the joint author of the four scientific papers between 1953 and 1954 (which he co-wrote with fellow scientist Francis Crick) that laid down the double helical structure of Deoxyribonucleic Acid (DNA), a megamolecule that is the fundamental substance in the process of *genetic replication. This discovery won Watson and Crick (with Maurice Wilkins) the Nobel Prize in physiology or medicine in 1962.*

During the 1960s, Watson became one of the most celebrated science writers, as he published his textbook *Molecular Biology of the Gene* in 1965, and his best-selling autobiographical book *The Double Helix* in 1968. Watson became the undisputed leading voice in the whole of American science. He epitomised the scientific creativity in the 20th century science, giving rise to molecular biology and its two applied offsets; 'Biotechnology' and the 'Human Genome Project'.

Jane Goodall

"Every individual matters. Every individual has a role to play. Every individual makes a difference."

This famous quote is by a lady who has been interested in animals all of her life. Dame Valerie Jane Goodall was born in London in 1934. Jane Goodall is the world's foremost authority on chimpanzees, having closely observed their behaviour for the past quarter century in the jungles of the *Gombe Game Reserve in Africa, living in the chimps'* environment and gaining their confidence as in one of her projects she said that:

"Chimpanzees have given me so much. The long hours spent with them in the forest have enriched my life beyond measure. What I have learnt from them has shaped my understanding of human behaviour, of our place in nature."

As a child she was given a lifelike chimpanzee toy named Jubilee by her mother. Jubilee started her early love of animals. Today, the toy still sits on her dresser in London. As she writes in her book, *Reason For Hope:* "My mother's friends were horrified by this toy, thinking it would frighten me and give me nightmares." Jane was a bright student as she is the one of only nine people to receive a PhD degree in Ethology without first obtaining a BA or B.Sc.

Were it not for fate, Goodall may have ended up being a secretary instead of the champion of animals as she now and went to the secretarial school and then had a series of jobs at the Oxford University and for a film studio that made documentary films until by chance a friend invited her to travel to Kenya. She saved her money by working as a waitress until she could afford to travel by boat to Kenya. She sailed from London to Africa on the passenger liner, The *Kenya Castle.* Two months after arriving there she met Louis Leakey, a famous, anthropologist and his wife, Mary.

Contributions and Achievements:

After a period of working with the Leakeys in the Uvalde Gorge, Leakey recognised in Goodall the right qualities to do an in depth study of *chimpanzees* in the *Gombe National Park in Tanzania*.

Dr. Goodall's research at Gombe Stream is best known to the scientific community for challenging two long-standing beliefs of the day: that only humans could construct and use tools, and that chimpanzees were passive vegetarians. While observing one chimpanzee feeding at a termite mound, she watched him repeatedly place stalks of grass into termite holes, then remove them from the hole covered with clinging termites, effectively "fishing" for termites. The chimps would also take twigs from trees and strip off the leaves to make the twig more effective, a form of object modification which is the rudimentary beginnings of tool making.

Humans had long distinguished us from the rest of the animal kingdom as "Man the Toolmaker". In response to Goodall's revolutionary findings, Louis Leakey wrote, "We must now redefine man, redefine tool, or accept chimpanzees as human!" Over the course of her study, Goodall found evidence of mental traits in chimpanzees, such as reasoned thought, abstraction, generalization, symbolic representation, and even the concept of self, all previously thought to be uniquely human abilities.

But the most disturbing thing was the tendency for aggression and violence within chimpanzee troops. Goodall observed dominant females deliberately killing the young of other females in the troop in order to maintain their dominance, sometimes going as far as *cannibalism*. These findings revolutionised contemporary knowledge of chimpanzee behaviour, and were further evidence of the social similarities between humans and chimpanzees, albeit it in a much darker manner.

Goodall also set herself apart from the traditional conventions of the time by naming the animals in her studies of primates, instead of assigning each a number. Numbering was a nearly universal practice at the time, and thought to be important in the removal of one's self from the potential for emotional attachment to the subject being studied.

Jane was the international recipient of the 1996 Caring Award for Scientific Achievements. She also received the National Geographic Society's prestigious Hubbard Medal 'for her extraordinary study of wild chimpanzees and for tirelessly defending the natural world we share. She has also appeared in an episode of Nickelodeon's animated series and is also a character in Irregular Web comic Steve and Terry theme. A parody of Goodall featured as a diamond-hoarding chimpanzee slave driver in an episode of The Simpsons.

Today, Jane Goodall spends much of her time lecturing, sharing her message of hope for the future and encouraging young people to make a difference in their world.

Jean Piaget

1896 – 1980

Jean Piaget was a Swiss psychologist who is known for conducting a systematic study of the acquisition of understanding in children. He is widely considered to be the most important figure in the 20th-century *developmental psychology.*

Born in 1896 in Neuchâtel, Switzerland, Jean Piaget's father, Arthur Piaget, taught *medieval literature at* the *University of Neuchâtel.* Piaget showed an early interest in Biology and the Natural World. He attended the *University of Neuchâtel,* and later, the *University of Zürich.*

Even as a young student, Piaget wrote two philosophical papers that were unfortunately rejected as adolescent thoughts.

It has been believed that no theoretical framework has had a bigger influence on developmental psychology than that of Jean Piaget. He founded the International Centre of Genetic Epistemology at Geneva and became its director. He made extraordinary contributions in various areas, including sociology, experimental psychology and scientific thoughts.

Contributions & Achievements:

Piaget took ideas from biology, psychology and philosophy and investiagated the method by which children learn about the world. He based his conclusions about child development on his observations and conversations with his own, as well as other children. By asking them ingenious and revealing questions about simple problems he had devised, he shaped a picture of their way of viewing the world by analysing their mistaken responses. He forumalated an outstandingly well-articulated and integrated *theory of cognitive development.*

Piaget was a highly prolific author who wrote about *70 books* and more than *100 articles* about *human psychology.* His theoretical conceptualisations have induced a vast amount of research.

Jean Piaget was honoured with the *Balzan Prize for Social and Political Sciences in 1979.* The following year, he died on September 16, 1980. He was 84 years old.

Jean-Baptiste Lamarck

1744 – 1829

Jean-Baptiste-Pierre-Antoine de Monet, Chevalier de Lamarck, more commonly known as *Jean-Baptiste Lamarck,* was a legendary French biologist, who advocated that *acquired characters are inheritable.*

Though his theory of heredity has been refuted by modern genetics and evolutionary theory, nevertheless Lamarck is widely regarded as one of the most influential naturalists and an important forerunner of evolution.

Born in Bazentin, Picardy, France in 1768 to an aristocrat father, Jean-Baptiste Lamarck started studying Botany, and issued his first work, *la Flore Française*", in 1778. The book gained him fame and with his good friend and naturalist Georges Buffon, he was made a member of the Academy of Sciences in 1779.

Contributions & Achievements:

Lamarck was apppointed an associate botanist in 1783. He soon gained worldwide acclaim after beginning a career in 1788 at the prestigious botanical garden, Jardin du Roi, Paris (now Jardin des Plantes). As the garden was reorganised in 1793, he gave some great ideas to set up the structure of the new *Museum of Natural History.*

The same year, Lamarck was selected as the professor of the Chair of *Invertebrate Zoology.*

Lamarck's brilliant contributions to science comprise of extraordinary work in Botany, Paleontology, Geology, Meteorology and Chemistry.

A few of his famous publications include: *Système des Animaux sans vertèbres* (1801) and *Recherche sur l'organisation des espèces (1802).* He was appointed a member of the *French Academy of Sciences in 1779.*

Lamarck went blind and died a poor man in Paris on December 18, 1829.

Jim Al-Khalili

Jim Al-Khalili is a *famous British physicist and author* of Iraqi descent. A professor of Theoretical Physics at the University of Surrey, Al-Khalili gained fame for writing a popular science book named *Blackholes, Wormholes* and *Time Machines*.

He often appears on several television shows to explain various scientific ideas.

Jim Al-Khalili was born in Baghdad in 1962. He had Iraqi father and an English mother. After studying physics at the University of Surrey, he acquired a B.Sc. degree in 1986.

He did his *Ph.D.* in Nuclear Reaction Theory in 1989. In the same year, he was awarded a *post-doctoral fellowship* at the University College London.

Contributions & Achievements:

After returning to Surrey in 1991, Jim Al-Khalili became an expert and notable author on *mathematical models of exotic atomic nuclei.*

As a prominent broadcaster, he frequently appears on television and radio. He has written *countless articles for the British press.*

Al-Khalili was honoured with the *Royal Society Michael Faraday Prize* for science communication in 2007.

He is also a member of the British *Council of Science and Engineering Advisory Group* as well as the *Royal Society Equality and Diversity Panel.*

He was appointed *Officer of the Order of the British Empire (OBE)* in 2008.

Jocelyn Bell Burnell

1943 - PRESENT

Entering the professional world as a woman has never been easy. It is not because women are inefficient or lack quick learning power, but simply because she is not a man. For ages, women have stayed and worked at their homes. Although today things have modernised to a great extent, the world still carries over some of these inferior feelings towards women. Jocelyn Bell Burnell is an exception to these feelings, setting a great example for the entire womenfolk. She is a bright and talented woman in one of the most male-dominated fields, Science. She is a *British astrophysicist* who is famous for her discovery of the *first radio pulsars* with her thesis supervisor *Antony Hewish,* for which *Hewish shared the Nobel Prize in Physics with Martin Ryle.*

Jocelyn Bell Burnell was born on July 15, 1943 in Belfast, Northen Island. Her father was an architect for the Armagh Observatory, where Jocelyn spent much of her time as a child. At a young age, she read a number of books on astronomy and her interest in the subject was encouraged by the staff of the Armagh Observatory. She attended the Lurgan College and went on to earn a Physics degree at the Glasgow University, Scotland in 1965. In 1969, she completed her Ph.D. from the *University of Cambridge,* where under the supervision of Antony Hewish, she also constructed and operated a *81.5 megahertz radio telescope.* She studied interplanetary scintillation of compact radio sources.

Contributions & Achievements:

In 1967, Bell, while analysing literally miles of print-outs from the telescope, noted a few unusual signals which she termed as "scruff". These "bits of scruff" seemed to indicate radio signals too fast and regular to come from quasars. Both Jocelyn and Hewish ruled out orbiting satellites, the French television signals, radar, finally even "little green men." Looking back at some papers in theoretical physics, they determined that these signals must have emerged from rapidly spinning, super-dense, collapsed stars. The media named these as *collapsed stars pulsars* and published the story.

In 1968, soon after her discovery, Bell married Martin Burnell (divorced in 1993). Her husband was a government worker, and his career took them to various parts of England. She worked part-time for many years, while raising her son, Gavin Burnell. During that period she began studying almost every wave spectrum in astronomy and gained an extraordinary breadth of experience. She held a junior teaching fellowship from 1970 to 1973 at the University of Southampton where she developed and calibrated a 1-10 million electron volt gamma-ray telescope. She also held research and teaching positions in x-ray astronomy at the Mullard Space Science Laboratory in London, and studied infrared astronomy in Edinburgh.

Jocelyn did not share the *Nobel Prize* awarded to Hewish for the discovery of *pulsars*, but has received numerous awards for her professional contributions. She was first chosen as a *fellow of the Royal Astronomical Society in 1969* and has served as its *Vice President*. Among many of her awards, she received the *Beatrice M. Tinsley Prize* from the *American Astronomical Society* in 1987 and the Herschel Medal from the Royal Astronomical Society in 1989. She also won the *Oppenheimer Prize* and The *Michelson Medal.*

She is currently a *Visiting Professor of Astrophysics* at the *University of Oxford* and a *Fellow of Mansfield College*. Also *Jocelyn is the current President of the Institute of Physics.*

Johannes Kepler

1571-1630

Johannes Kepler is one name that will always be remembered in the field of *astronomy*. He was the chief founder of *contemporary astronomy* and also a *great mathematician* and *astrologer*. The German astronomer was the first person to *explain planetary motion.* His three laws on planetary motion were codified by later astronomers based on his works *Astronomia nova, Harmonices Mundi,* and *Epitome of Copernican Astronomy.* They also served as the basis for *Isaac Newton's theory of universal gravitation*. Moreover his publication *Stereometrica Doliorum* formed the foundation of *integral calculus,* and he also made *imperative advances in geometry.*

Johannes Kepler was born on December 27, 1571 in Weil der Stadt in Swabia, in south-west Germany. He had six siblings, three of which died already at an early age. His father, Heinrich Kepler was a soldier and mother, Katharina Guldenmann was a healer and herbalist. His Grandfather Sebald Kepler, had been Lord Mayor of the town but by the time Kepler was born, the family had become very poor. As a child, Kepler led a very unfortunate life; recovering from smallpox at the age of four with crippled hands and eyesight permanently weakened. He also lost his father when he was just five years old.

In 1576, the family moved to Leonberg where Johannes began his schooling first in the *German School* and then the *Latin School.* In 1583, he passed the exam in Stuttgart and the following year, he went to Seminar Adelberg, a convent school. After two years he was accepted at a higher seminar in Maulbronn, also a convent school. Upon achieving a scholarship he joined the University of Tuebingen in 1589, where he studied *philosophy* under *Vitus Müller* and *theology* under *Jacob Heerbrand.*

Johannes excelled in mathematics and proved himself as a *skilled astrologer, forecasting horoscopes for fellow students.* Under the guidance of Michael Maestlin, Tübingen's professor of mathematics, he gained knowledge about both the Ptolemaic System and the Copernican System of Planetary Motion. He became a Copernican at that time. In 1594, shortly before finishing his studies, he went to Graz as teacher of mathematics and astronomy and remained there until 1600.

Contributions & Achievements:

In 1600 Kepler met the great mathematician and court astronomer, Tycho Brahe in Prague. Tycho Brahe was working for Emperor Rudolf II and had the most accurate empiric data and precise measuring instruments of his time. Kepler became his assistant and saw the opportunity to test his astronomical theories empirically. The teamwork of the two men was disturbed because of differing point of views; Brahe was more convinced of the geocentric world view and Kepler more of the heliocentric one. Both of them worked together on planets and Brahe also gave Kepler the task to define the motion of the planet, Mars.

During 1601, the *emperor, Rudolph* II appointed him to succeed his patron as *imperial mathematician.* The first works completed by him at Prague were, nevertheless homage to the astrological proclivities of the emperor. In *De fundamentis astrologiae certioribus* (1602), he declared his purpose of preserving and purifying the grain of truth which he believed the science to contain. In 1604, Astronomia pars Optica appeared, in which he treated both atmospheric refraction and lenses. In 1606, he published *De Stella Nova* which was about the new star that had appeared in 1604.

Five years later, in 1609, he published *Astronomia Nova,* which contained his first two laws on planetary motion. In 1612, he moved to Linz where he served as a teacher at the district school and provided astrological and astronomical services. In 1619, he published the *Harmonice Mundi* where we find his third law besides his derivation of the heliocentric distances of the planets and their periods from considerations of musical harmony.

Kepler married twice in his life. His first marriage was to Barbara Müller on April 27, 1597. Later after the death of his wife, he remarried on October 30, 1613 to Susanna Reuttinger.

He died in Regensburg, Germany on November 15, 1630. Like many geniuses, Kepler has never known fame or fortune, but his determination and persistence led to many discoveries that enable us to understand the universe today.

John Bardeen

1908 – 1991

John Bardeen was an eminent American physicist, who won the *Nobel Prize twice.* In 1956, with fellow scientists, William B. Shockley and Walter H. Brattainhe, Bardeen shared the award for the invention of the *transistor*. He received the award for the second time in 1972, with *Leon N. Cooper* and *John R. Schrieffer,* for formulating the *theory of superconductivity.* Bardeen thus revolutionised the fields of *electronics* and *magnetic resonance imaging.*

Born in Madison, Wisconsin in 1908, John Bardeen's father was a Professor of Anatomy and the first Dean of the Medical School at the University of Wisconsin. He acquired a BS degree in electrical engineering from the same university in 1928, and after one year, his MS degree in 1929.

Following a few years of research work in geophysics, Bardeen took another degree in mathematical physics from the Princeton University, receiving a Ph.D. in 1936.

Contributions & Achievements:

After years of research work at the universities of Minnesota and Harvard, in addition to the *Naval Ordonnance Lab* in Washington DC, John Bardeen finally joined the *solid state physics group at Bell Labs in New Jersey in 1945*. He developed an interest in semiconductor research and collaborated with Brattain and Shockley to discover the transistor effect in semiconductors in 1947. His efforts laid the foundation for the *modern age of electronics and computers.*

Bardeen left Bell Labs and accepted a teaching position at the *University of Illinois* in 1951. At this place, he worked with the Cooper and Schrieffer to formulate the first *successful microscopic theory of superconductivity,* which was later termed as the *BCS theory.* Bardeen was awarded the *Nobel Prize twice* for his efforts, and he remains the only person in history to have *two prizes in the same domain.*

He revolutionised the fields of *electrical engineering* and *solid slate physics. The transistor is often recognised as the most influential invention of the 20th century.*

Bardeen died of heart disease on January 30, 1991 in Boston, Massachusetts, where he had come to Brigham and Women's Hospital for medical treatment. He was buried in the Forest Hill Cemetery. John Bardeen was named by the *Life Magazine* to be one among the *100 most influential people of the 20th century.*

John Dalton

The scientific field has witnessed the emergence of many great physicists and chemists; but it is incomplete without the mention of the great British chemist, meteorologist and physicist, John Dalton. His tremendous efforts led to the evolution of the *modern atomic theory.* He was the first person to *record colour blindness*. He also carried out his research to explain the *shortage of colour perception.*

Dalton was born into a modest Quaker family in Cumberland, England around 5th September, 1766. He got his early education from his father and his teacher, John Fletcher of the Quakers' school at Eaglesfield, on whose retirement in 1778 he himself began teaching. He spent most of his life teaching and giving public lectures. After serving ten years at a Quaker boarding school in Kendal in 1793, he took another teaching position in the rapidly increasing city of Manchester. There he taught math and natural philosophy at the 'New College' until 1800, when he resigned due to worsening financial condition of the college. Afterwards he gave private tuitions for mathematics and natural philosophy.

Contributions & Achievements:

Most of the credit of Dalton's interests in mathematics and meteorology goes to Elihu Robinson, an experienced meteorologist and instrument maker who greatly influenced his initial years of life. At Kendal, Dalton proposed solutions of problems and questions on various subjects to the Gentlemen's and Ladies' Diaries, and starting in 1787, he maintained a meteorological diary in which during the succeeding 57 years, he entered over 200,000 observations.

His first separate publication was *Meteorological Observations and Essays* (1793), which explained many of his later discoveries; but in spite of the originality of its content, the book met with only a limited attention. Another work by him was published in 1801 as Elements of English Grammar.

In 1794, John joined the *Manchester Literary and Philosophical Society,* which provided him with an exciting academic environment and laboratory services. After few weeks, he presented his first paper on 'Extraordinary facts relating to the vision of colours' before the society. In this paper, he explained that the shortage in colour perception was caused by discolouration of the liquid medium of the eyeball. He himself was a victim of colour blindness and was the first one to discover the concept. As a result, 'Daltonism' became synonymous with *colour blindness.*

Contributions & Achievementss:

Dalton's greatest interest was in meteorology and he maintained daily records of local temperature, wind, humidity and atmospheric pressure using instruments that he devised himself. By 1800, he was appointed the secretary of the Manchester Literary and Philosophical Society and published a series of papers entitled 'Experimental Essays on the Constitution of Mixed Gases; on the force of steam or vapour of water and other liquids in different temperatures, both in Torricellian vacuum and in air; on evapouration; and on the expansion of gases by heat.'

In 1803, he published his gas law which is now known as 'Dalton's law.' In this law, he basically stated that the total pressure exerted by a gaseous mixture is equal to the sum of the partial pressures of each individual component in a gas mixture.

He calculated atomic weights of elements and assembled them in a table which consisted of six elements namely hydrogen, oxygen, nitrogen, carbon, sulpfur, and phosphorus. He calculated these weights from percentage compositions of compounds using an arbitrary system to determine the probable atomic structure of each compound.

John Dalton's Atomic theory has three principles that remain relatively unchanged. First, Elements are made of the smallest particles called atoms. Second, all atoms for a particular element are identical. Third, atoms of different elements can be hold apart by their atomic weight. Fourth, atoms of different elements can combine in a *chemical reaction* to form *chemical compounds* in *fixed ratios.* Finally, atoms cannot be created, destroyed, or divided as they are the smallest particles of matter. Even though some of its postulates were opposed by many scholars and scientists, Dalton's Atomic Theory still holds a lot of significance as it created a basis for current science.

Dalton died of a stroke on July 27, 1844 and was buried in Manchester in Ardwick cemetery.

John Locke

1632 – 1704

John Locke was an English philosopher and physician, often considered as one of the greatest and *most influential Enlightenment thinkers in history.*

Born in Somerset, England in 1932, John Locke's father was a prominent country lawyer.

He was raised in a rural house in Belluton. Locke attended the famous Westminster School in London, and was later admitted to Christ Church, Oxford.

He acquired a bachelor's degree in 1656 and a master's degree in 1658. He also obtained a bachelor of medicine in 1674.

Contributions & Achievements:

John Locke is widely considered to be one of the greatest English philosophers and a leading figure in the fields of epistemology, metaphysics and political philosophy.

He also made crucial contributions to education, theology, medicine, physics, economics, and politics. Locke's empiricist epistemology (he was the founder of empiricist theory of knowledge) inspired Berkeley, Hume, and the later years of empiricism.

Locke's political philosophy is often noted with shaping both the American Constitution and the French Revolution and laid the groundwork for liberal political thought. He was the first person to explain the self through a continuity of consciousness. *He proposed that the mind was a blank slate or tabula rasa.* Some of the Locke's most noted works are “An Essay Concerning Human Understanding”, “Two Treatises of Government”, and “A Letter Concerning Toleration”.

Locke never married in his lifetime. He died in 1704 at the age of 72. He was buried in the churchyard of the village of High Laver, Essex.

John Logie Baird

1888 - 1946

John Logie Baird is a very famous Scottish inventor who was born in 1888 in Scotland. *He played a vital role in the invention of the television and it was his invention* of *photomechanical television that broadcasted the transmission live for the first time ever.* He studied at the University of Glasgow and also at the Royal Technical College. It was due to his unstable health that he could not participate in World War I and he was enforced to give up his electric engineering post. After that he tried out many activities and tried to figure out his areas of interest as he had declared himself as a "Professional Amateur".

It was after his nervous breakdown that he started paying attention to electronics. *Marconi's explanation about the travelling of radio waves* was his area of concentration. He was almost sure that visual signals could also be transmitted through the same process. With his firm believe he started working on his project. The basic design of Baird contained a *scanning disk* named *Nipkow disk* after its German inventor, Paul Nipkow, which was developed in 1884. This device was made up of a disk made out of cardboard that had square holes in it in series, spirally placed. The Nipkow disk scanned light and dark areas when it spun with the *photoelectric cell.* This process converted into electrical signals. When two such disks worked in synchronisation, the signals were again translated into *visual images.*

Contributions & Achievements:

Baird made innovations in this idea of Nipkow and added a feature to it which could transmit signals through electromagnetic waves instead of cable wires. The innovation was not appreciated and financed much by the investors. Throughout this time, Baird took odd jobs, such as of a salesman for razor blade and a shoe shiner just to earn enough money to support himself and buy his tools. Many of his inventions involved the use of household items like string, bicycle lamps, cake tin and knitting needles etc. Finally on October 2, 1925, Baird accomplished in transmitting the picture of the dummy of ventriloquist from his attic's one end to another. He got really excited and ran to the nearest shop to convince a boy to be a part of his television transmission. This invention gave fame to Baird in a jiffy and also arouse interest of the investors. A television signal was sent by him from London to Glasgow in 1927 and from London to New York later in 1928. The only problem was this design produced poor quality image. Vladimir Zworykin's design of cathode ray tube substituted Baird's design. Baird still helped in developing improved designs of televisions. He also helped with the *coloured television* and *large and wide screen projection* which he thought would later be used for *movie projection for public.* Baird passed away in 1946 when he was 58.

John Napier

John Napier was a very famous mathematician of his time and he was born in 1550 in Edinburgh, Scotland. His father was Sir Archibald Napier. Logarithms and the decimals' modern notations were introduced by him. He was very bright and he got admitted in the University of St. Andrews only when he was thirteen years old. It is also said that he had probably also studied at some universities in France and Italy.

Napier came back to his homeland by 1571 and got married to Elizabeth Stirling, the very next year. At the castle of Gartnes, Napier had enough time to explore his interests in the field of religious politics, agriculture and mathematics.

Contributions & Achievements:

A Calvinist was set to drive away Catholicism from Scotland at any cost. There was a scheme named as *Spanish Blanks* against which Napier revolted with a certain book called *A Plaine Discovery* of the Whole Revelation of St. John (1594). Napier set up four new kinds of weapons to make the struggle more powerful. The weapons included an artillery piece, a kind of battle vehicle that was covered with plates of metal and had tiny opening for emitting odious smoke and firepower and two kinds of burning mirrors. The vehicle was driven by men inside.

Soon the Catholic or Spanish conquest was over and that led Napier to get back to his work. He promoted the use of common salt and manure for soil improvement in agriculture. In math, he made remarkable discoveries that were accurate and were accepted all over the world. *His technique of calculation of log got published in 1614 Mirifici logarithmorum canonis description.* The technique was found to be really accurate that his work was translated into different languages and also widely printed. It helped in the *trigonometric calculations* in *astronomy* and *navigation*. His work about the computation of logarithm in *1920 Mirifici logarithmorum canonis construction* was published even after his death.

A copy of Napier's work of 1614 was sent to a professor of Gresham College, Henry Briggs. Briggs made Napier's method even easier by setting log of 1 at zero. Napier agreed with it but left the responsibility of setting up the new logarithm table *by Briggs' plan* on *Briggs*. It was published in 1624 and was called the *table of common logarithms.*

For more than 20 years, Napier worked on a very complex subject that held a great value to physical science. A device named N*apier's rods or bones* shows creativeness of his mind in the field of mathematics. Many mathematical functions like multiplication and division could be done mechanically. This device helped in analog computers and slide rules. *Rabdologiae; seu Numerationes per Virgulas libri duo* is the work published about his work in two volumes in 1617. He passed away the same year on the 4th of April.

John Needham

John Turberville Needham, more commonly known as John Needham, was an English naturalist and Roman Catholic cleric. He was the first clergyman to be appointed as a *Fellow of the Royal Society of London. He is also noted for his theory of spontaneous generation and the scientific evidence, he had presented to support it.*

Born in London in 1713, John Turbeville Needham was a Catholic and he did become a priest. He was in fact ordained in 1738. *However, he preferred to spend his time as a teacher and tutor.*

Contributions & Achievements:

John Needham established *Académie impériale* et royale des Sciences et Belles-Lettres de Bruxelles in 1773 and remained its director until 1780. He was made a Fellow of the Royal Society of London in 1768. He carried out microscopical observations with Buffon in 1748.

Needham later conducted a learned correspondence with Bonnet and Spallanzani on the issue of generation.

He faced harsh criticisms from Voltaire, because he had tried to establish that tiny microscopic animals, or 'anguilles' in his own words, can be developed spontaneously by natural forces, yet in a sealed container.

Voltaire, who firmly believed in pre-existing germs, thought that Needham's ideas could possibly create much controversy as they appeared to endorse materialism and atheism.

Needham also made important contributions to Botany and explained the mechanics of the Pollen.

John Needham died on December 30, 1781. He was 68 years old.

John Ray

1627 – 1705

John Ray was a highly *influential English naturalist* and *botanist* whose contributions to *taxonomy* are considered groundbreaking and historic. He is also well-known in the world of botany for the establishment of species as the ultimate unit of taxonomy.

Born in 1627 in a small village of Black Notley, Essex, John Ray's father was a blacksmith. Ray entered the Cambridge University at the young age of sixteen.

Contributions & Achievements:

John Ray was selected a *Fellow of Trinity College in 1649*. However, he lost the position 13 years later when, in 1662, he declined to take the oath to the Act of Uniformity after the Restoration. With full support of his former student and fellow naturalist, Francis Willoughby, Ray made several trips throughout Europe with him, carrying out research in the fields of Botany and Zoology.

Ray formulated the fundamental principles of *plant classification into cryptogams, monocotyledons and dicotyledons* in his landmark works 'Catalogus plantarum Angliae' (1670) and "Methodus plantarum nova" (1682). Other major publications of Ray include 'Historia generalis plantarum' (3 volumes, 1686-1704) and 'The Wisdom of God Manifested in the Works of the Creation' (1691), both of which became quite influential during the time.

The zoological contributions of Ray include the development of the most *natural pre-Linnaean classification* of the animal kingdom.

He was appointed a *Fellow of the Royal Society in 1667.* Ray endorsed scientific empiricism as compared to the deductive rationalism of the scholastics.

In his later years, Ray moved to his native village, where he remained until his death in 1705. He was 77 years old. *The Ray Society was established in his honour in 1844.*

John von Neumann

John von Neumann was a pioneer of the application of *operator theory* to *quantum mechanics,* in the development of functional analysis. Along with Teller and Stanislaw Ulam, Von Neumann worked out the key steps in Nuclear Physics involved in Thermonuclear Reactions and the Hydrogen Bomb. *Von Neumann wrote about 150 published papers in his life; 60 in pure mathematics, 20 in physics and 60 in applied mathematics.* His last work, published in book form as *The Computer and the Brain,* gives an indication of the direction of his interests at the time of his death.

John von Neumann was born on December 28, 1903. He was a Hungarian-American mathematician who made major contributions to a vast range of fields. The eldest of the three brothers, Von Neumann was born *Neumann Janos Lajos*. Von Neumann's ancestors had originally immigrated to Hungary from Russia. John was a child prodigy who showed an aptitude for languages, memorisation, and mathematics. By the age of six, he could exchange jokes in Classical Greek, memorise telephone directories and displayed prodigious mental calculation abilities. He received his Ph.D. in mathematics from Pázmány Peter University in Budapest. That time he was 22 years of age. At the same time, he earned his diploma in chemical engineering from the ETH Zurich in Switzerland. John Neumann married twice. He married Mariette Kövesi in 1930, just before emigrating to the United States. They had one daughter. He then divorced her in 1937 and married Klari Dan in 1938.

Contributions & Achievements:

In 1937, Von Neumann became a *naturalised citizen of the US.* This was after migrating with his mother and *brothers. In 1938*, von Neumann was awarded the *Bôcher Memorial Prize* for his work in analysis.

Von Neumann also created the field of cellular automata without the aid of computers, constructing the first self-replicating automata with pencil and graph paper. Throughout his life, Von Neumann had a respect and admiration for business and government leaders; something which was often at variance with the inclinations of his scientific colleagues.

Von Neumann's interest in meteorological prediction led him to manipulating the environment by spreading colourants on the polar ice caps to enhance absorption of solar radiation, thereby raising the global temperatures.

Von Neumann's principal contribution to the atomic bomb itself was in the concept and design of the explosive lenses needed to compress the plutonium core of the Trinity Test Device. Von Neumann's hydrogen bomb work was also played out in the realm of computing, where he and Stanislaw Ulam developed simulations on Von Neumann's digital computers for the hydrodynamic computations. During this time, he contributed to the development of the *Monte Carlo method,* which allowed complicated problems to be approximated using random numbers.

Von Neumann's first significant contribution to economics was the *Minimax Theorem of 1928.* This theorem establishes that in certain zero sum games with perfect information. Basically, there exists a strategy for each player which allows both players to minimise their maximum losses.

An astoundingly creative mathematician, John von Neumann has played a rather important role in *post-war economic theory.*

John Neumann died on February 8, 1957 (aged 53) in Washington, D.C., United States.

Jonas Salk

1914 - 1995

"*Life is an error-making and an error-correcting process*, and nature in marking man's papers will grade him for wisdom as measured both by survival and by the quality of life of those who survive."

This famous saying is by *Jonas Salk,* born in New York City on October 28, 1914, who is among the most respected medical scientists of the century. Though his first words were reported to be *dirt,* his early thoughts were not on studying *germs* but on going into *law*. He became interested in biology and chemistry, however, and decided to go into research. He went to the New York University medical school for training.

While attending medical school at the New York University, Salk was invited to spend a year researching *influenza*. The virus that causes flu had only recently been discovered and young Salk was eager to learn if the virus could be deprived of its ability to infect, while still giving immunity to the illness. Salk succeeded in this attempt, which became the basis of his later works on *polio*.

Contributions & Achievements:

His actual work to cure polio started when in America in the 1950s, summertime was a time of concern and worry for many parents as this was the season when children by the thousands became infected with the crippling disease, polio. This burden of fear was lifted forever when it was announced that Dr. Jonas Salk had developed a vaccine against the disease. The vaccine proved successful as everybody who received the test vaccine began producing antibodies against the virus so that nobody else became inflicted with polio and no side effects were observed.

Jonas Salk published the results in the Journal of the *American Medical Association,* the following year and a nationwide testing was made.

It was during this time that worst polio eruption happened. It was Salk's former mentor, Thomas Francis Jr. that helped and directed the *mass vaccination of schoolchildren.* Salk became world-famous overnight, but his discovery was the result of many years of painstaking research. In 1947, Salk accepted an appointment to the *University of Pittsburgh Medical School.* While working there with the National Foundation for Infantile Paralysis, Salk saw an opportunity to develop a vaccine against polio, and devoted himself to this work for the next eight years.

The March of Dimes, hoping to boost publicity and donations to fund vaccination programs, praised Salk to the point of offending his colleagues. He had applied the findings of others in a successful made the public blind to that. bid to prevent disease. Other researchers and doctors grumbled that he hadn't find anything new; he had just applied what was there. But the timing of his successful vaccine was at the peak of polio's devastation period.

In the years after his discovery, many supporters, in particular, the National Foundation 'helped him build his dream of a research complex for the investigation of biological phenomena. It was called the Salk Institute for Biological Studies and opened in 1963 at California. Salk believed that the institution would help new and upcoming scientists along their careers as he said tohimself', 'I thought how nice it would be if a place like this existed and I was invited to work there.' This was something that Salk was deprived of early in his life, but due to his Achievementss, was able to provide for future scientists.

Under Salk's direction, the Institute began research activities in and gradually expanded its faculty and the areas of their research interests. Salk's personal research activities included multiple sclerosis and autoimmune diseases, cancer immunology, improved manufacture and standardization of killed poliovirus vaccine, and another developments in which Salk also engaged in research to develop a vaccine for more recent plague, AIDS. To further this research, he co-founded The Immune Response Corporation, to search for a vaccine, and patented Remune, an immune-based therapy.

In 1966, Salk described his ambitious plan for the creation of a kind of Socratic academy where the supposedly alienated two cultures of science and humanism will have a favourable atmosphere for cross-fertilization. President Ronald Reagan proclaimed that day to be *Jonas Salk* Day making people *realize* that Salk always had a passion for science. It was because of this that he finally chose medicine over law as his career goal. Even after his great discovery, he continued to undertake vital studies and medical research to benefit his fellowman. Under his vision and leadership, the Salk Institute for Biological Studies has been in the forefront of basic biological research, reaping further benefits for mankind and medical science.

The New York Times referred to him as the 'Father of Biophilosophy'. As a biologist, he believes that his science is on the frontier of tremendous new discoveries and as a philosopher, he is of the view that humanists and artists have joined the scientists to achieve an understanding of man in all his physical, mental and spiritual complexity. Such interchanges might lead, he would hope, to a new and important school of thinkers he would designate as biophilosopher.

His definition of a 'bio-philosopher' is "Someone who draws upon the scriptures of nature, recognising that we are the product of the process of evolution, and understands that we have become the process itself, through the emergence and evolution of our consciousness, our awareness, our capacity to imagine and anticipate the future, and to choose from among various alternatives.

Salk died at the age of 80 on June 23, 1995. *A monument at the Institute with a statement from Salk captures his vision, "Hope lies in dreams, in imagination and in the courage of those who dare to make dreams into reality."*

Joseph Banks

1743 – 1820

Sir Joseph Banks was an eminent *English naturalist, explorer and botanist, noted for his promotion of natural sciences.* He also remains the longest serving *President of the Royal Society of London.*

Born in London on January 4, 1743 in a rich family, Joseph Banks inherited a sizeable fortune when his father, William Banks, a famous doctor, died. He took admission in *Christ Church, Oxford,* in 1760. When he left the college in 1763, he had an extensive knowledge of natural history, particularly of Botany.

Contributions & Achievements:

Joseph Banks was selected a *Fellow of the Royal Society in 1766.* He *joined Captain Cook on his 1763 voyage around the world.* Dr. Solander, a friend of Banks, also accompanied him as a naturalist. After their return, both wanted to publish a botanical work as they had acquired huge collections of natural objects from the expedition. Due to Solander's unexpected death, they were unable to complete it. Banks also toured Iceland in 1772.

He became the *President of the Royal Society in 1777,* where he remained until 1820. He was known as a prominent endorser of travellers and scientific men. Many voyages of discovery were approved and carried out under his supervision. He was the first person to *introduce the Western world to acacia, mimosa, eucalyptus and Banksia, a genus named after him. About 80 other species of plants were also named after him.* Banks also established the fact that *marsupial mammals were more primitive than placental mammals.*

Joseph Banks was knighted in 1781. He was made a member of the *Privy Council in 1797.* He was also appointed an *associate of the Institute of France In 1802.* Two of his most famous publications include

"Short Account of the Cause of the Disease in Corn called the Blight, the Mildew, and the Rust," (1803) and "Circumstances Relative to Metino Sheep" (1809).

Joseph Banks died in London in 1820. He was 77 years old and left no family. Banks was buried at St Leonard's Church, Heston.

Joseph Priestley

1733 - 1804

Joseph Priestley was an English scientist, philosopher, theologian and clergyman who authored more than 150 publications. He is noted for his groundbreaking contributions to *experimental chemistry*, *electricity* and the *chemistry of gases*, as well as his extraordinary work regarding *liberal, political and religious thoughts.*

Born at Birstall Fieldhead, England, Joseph Priestley proved to be a very intelligent child from an early age. *He learned mathematics, logics, metaphysics and natural philosophy.*

Priestley also learnt more than six different languages including Latin, Hebrew and Greek.

Joseph Priestley is highly regarded for his work with the *chemistry of gases. As a friend of Benjamin Franklin, Priestley contacted him regarding his theories of electricity.* He later experimented with distinguishing various types of 'air'.

Before him, scientists thought that the air on, the Earth consisted of only carbondioxide and hydrogen. Priestley brought *10 more gases* to this list, such as *nitrogen, hydrogen chloride, carbon monoxide, nitrous oxide* and *oxygen.* He also invented *soda water.*

Priestley wrote several *theological, philosophical* and *political essays.* He made the English press and government furious with his theories regarding '*Rational Christianity*' and '*Laissez-Faire Economics*'.

Priestley, along with his family, narrowly escaped hundreds of raging protesters who attacked their homes in 1791.

Joseph Priestley fled to the United States in 1794. He died in Northumberland Pennsylvania on Feb 6, 1804. He was buried at Riverview Cemetery in Northumberland, Pennsylvania.

Justus von Liebig

Justus von Liebig was a German chemist, who is widely credited as one of the founders of agricultural chemistry. He made crucial contributions to the analysis of organic compounds, and, in his early years, also published several works on the use of inorganic fertilizers in several languages. He discovered that nitrogen was an essential plant nutrient, and presented his famous Law of the Minimum which explained the effect of individual nutrients on crops.

Born in Darmstadt, Germany on May 12, 1803, Justus von Liebig's father was a chemical manufacturer whose shop had a small laboratory.

Young Liebig loved to perform experiments at the place. After learning pharmacy for about six months, he acquired a degree in chemistry from the Prussian University of Bonn. Liebig received his doctorate from the University of Erlangen in Bavaria in 1822.

Contributions & Achievements:

Liebig worked on the serious *explosive silver fulminate, a salt of fulminic acid.* During the same time, the German chemist Friedrich Wöhler was also studying cyanic acid. Liebig and Wöhler *collaborated to establish that cyanic acid and fulminic acid were two different compounds having the same composition.*

The concept of 'isomerism' was later recognised by the Swedish chemist Jöns Jacob Berzelius.

Liebig revolutionised the organic analysis using a five-bulb device called the "Kaliapparat". He understated the importance of humus in plant nutrition and maintained that plants feed upon nitrogen compounds, carbon dioxide from air, and some minerals found in the soil.

He was the first person the invent a nitrogen-based fertilizer. Liebig also devised the Law of the Minimum. Liebig was one of the true forefathers of modern agriculture.

Justus von Liebig was made a baron in 1845. He died on April 18, 1873. Liebig was buried in the Alter Südfriedhof, Munich.

Karl Landsteiner

1868 – 1943

Karl Landsteiner was an Austrian-born American immunologist, physician and pathologist. He was awarded the *Nobel Prize in 1930* for *Physiology or Medicine* for detecting the major *blood groups and creating* the *ABO system of blood typing* that revolutionised the process of *blood transfusion* and *medical practice* related to it.

Born in 1868 in Vienna, Austria to a journalist father, Karl Landsteiner was a bright student who was allowed to study medicine when he was merely 17 years old. He acquired a degree in medicine from the University of Vienna. Landsteiner envisioned that the future of medicine was in research, so he preferred to become a *research scientist* rather than an *ordinary medical practitioner.*

Contributions & Achievements:

Karl Landsteiner was the first biologist to identify *different blood types and to sort out blood into groups.* Before him, scientists thought that the blood of every person was the same. *Blood transfusion was often considered dangerous.* When it did not work, it was believed that the blood from the donor, 'clumped together' in the recipient's body and resulted in his death. Landsteiner demonstrated that there are certain differences in the structure of human blood types.

After working hard for almost one year testing several blood samples, Karl Landsteiner announced in 1901 that *there were three major human blood groups: A, B and C (which was later called O).* One year later in 1902, Landsteiner's three fellow scientists discovered a fourth blood type, named AB.

The role of Landsteiner's contributions in medicine is crucial and thousands of lives were saved in hospitals during World War I, and are still being saved to this day. Blood types are used by the police and criminologists to solve crimes by examining blood samples at crime scenes.

Karl Landsteiner was a notoriously private person who disliked publicity and rarely gave interviews and speeches, although much in demand. *He became a naturalised United States citizen in 1929.*

Landsteiner died of a heart attack in 1943, while still performing his duties at his laboratory at the age of 75. He was honoured with a *Lasker Award* in 1946, three years after his death.

Katharine Burr Blodgett

1898 - 1979

American scientist, Katharine Burr Blodgett is known for numerous important contributions to the field of *industrial chemistry.* She is mainly acknowledged for her invention of the *colour gauge* and *non-reflecting* or *'invisible' glass.*

Born in Schenectady, New York on January 10, 1898, Katharine or Katie (her nickname) was the second child of Katharine Burr and George Blodgett, a patent lawyer for the General Electric Company. Her father was killed only a few weeks before she was born. Her father's death left more than sufficient amount of wealth to the family. After Katie's birth, the family moved to New York City, then to France in 1901, and then back to New York City in 1912. Here she completed her schooling from the Rayson School and developed an early interest in mathematics. She completed high school at the age of fifteen and earned a scholarship to Bryn Mawr College receiving her B.A. degree in 1917.]

Contributions & Achievements:

Her interest in physics began when she attended college. After college, Blodgett decided that a career in scientific research would allow her to further pursue her interest in both mathematics and physics. During her vacations, Katie travelled to upstate New York in search of employment opportunities at the Schenectady GE plant. Some of her father's former colleagues in Schenectady introduced Katie to research chemist Irving Langmuir. While showing his laboratory, Irving Lengmuir recognised Katie's aptitude and advised her to continue her scientific education. Following his advice she went on to pursue master's degree in science and was the first woman to be ever awarded a doctorate in physics from Cambridge University.

After her masters, she became the first woman to be hired as a scientist at GE. Langmuir encouraged her to participate in some of his earlier discoveries. First, he put her on the task of perfecting tungsten filaments in electric lamps (the work for which he had received a patent in 1916). He later asked Katie to concentrate her studies on surface chemistry. Her most important contribution came from her independent research on an oily substance that Langmuir had developed in the lab.

The then existing methods for measuring this unusual substance, were only accurate to a few thousandths of an inch but Katie's way proved to be accurate to about one millionth of an inch. Her new discovery of measuring transparent objects led to her invention of non-reflecting glass in 1938. This invisible glass proved to be a very effective device for physicists, chemists, and metallurgists. It has been put to use in many consumer products from picture frames to camera lenses and has also been exceptionally helpful in optics.

During the Second World War, Katie made another outstanding breakthrough: the *smoke screens.* The smoke screens saved many lives by covering the troops, thereby protecting them from the exposure of toxic smoke.

Katie's work was acknowledged by many awards, including the *Garvan Medal* in 1951. She earned honorary degrees from the Elmira College in 1939, Brown University in 1942, Western College in1942, and Russell Sage College in 1944. She was nominated to be part of the *American Physical Society* and was a member of the *Optical Society of America.*

Katharine Burr Blodgett died in her home on October 12, 1979.

Konrad Lorenz

"Every man gets a narrower and narrower field of knowledge in which he must be an expert in order to compete with other people. The specialist knows more and more about less and less and finally knows everything about nothing."

"Truth in science can be defined as the working hypothesis best suited to open the way to the next better one."

The above quotations reflect the intellectual thinking of the great *Austrian zoologist, animal psychologist,* and *ornithologist, Konrad Zacharias Lorenz.* His exceptional work on animal behaviour earned him the *Nobel Prize in Physiology or Medicine in 1973*, which he shared with Nikolaas Tinbergen and Karl von Frisch. Lorenz examined animals in their natural environments and concluded that instinct plays a key role in animal behaviour. This observation challenged behavioural animal psychology, which defined all behaviour as learned. He is the author of several books, some of which, such as King Solomon's Ring and On Aggression became very popular during his time.

Konrad Zacharias Lorenz was brought up in Vienna and at the family's summer estate in Altenberg, a village on the Danube River. He was the younger son of Adolf Lorenz, a successful and wealthy orthopedic surgeon, and Emma Lecher Lorenz, a physician who assisted her husband. From a very early age Konrad was fond of keeping and observing animals.

Lorenz completed his schooling from one of Vienna's best secondary schools. He graduated from the University of Vienna as Doctor of Medicine (MD) in 1928 and was appointed an assistant professor at the Institute of Anatomy until 1935. He also began studying zoology, in which he was awarded a Ph.D. degree in 1933 by the same university.

Contributions & Achievements:

From 1935 to 1938, he made studies of geese and jackdaws (many of his significant scientific papers are based on this work). From his observations Lorenz established the concept of imprinting, the process by which an animal follows an object, normally its biological mother. He found that for a short time after hatching, chicks are genetically inclined to identify their mother's sound and appearance and thereby form a permanent bond with her.

Lorenz also put forward an innate releasing mechanism theory. He alleged that an animal's innate behaviour pattern ("innate releasing mechanism") will remain dormant until a stimulating event ("releaser") prompts it.

In 1940 he was appointed as the professor of psychology at the University of Königsberg. World War II (1939-1945) soon interrupted his academic career. He served as a doctor in the German army until his capture by the Russians in 1944. Four years after his release, he returned to Altenberg (his family home) and wrote the popular account of his work, translated as King Solomon's Ring (1949), which was followed by Man Meets Dog (1950). The Max Planck Society established the Lorenz Institute for Behavioural Physiology in Buldern, Germany, during 1950. In 1958, Lorenz transferred to the Max Planck Institute for Behavioural Physiology in Seewiesen.

In 1969, he became the first person to receive the *Prix Mondial Cino* Del Duca. In 1973, he became a *Nobel Prize Laureate* in *Physiology or Medicine* "for discoveries in individual and social behaviour patterns" with Nikolaas Tinbergen and Karl von Frisch.

Lorenz left the Max Planck Institute in 1973 but continued his research and writing in Altenberg and Grünau im Almtal in Austria.

Konrad Lorenz died on February 27, 1989, in Altenberg.

Lee De Forest

1873 – 1961

*T*he American inventor and electrical engineer, Lee De Forest is credited for inventing the *Audion, a vacuum tube* that takes moderately weak electrical signals and amplifies. them. *The device helped AT&T established coast-to-coast phone service, and it was also used in everything from radios to televisions to the first computers.*

Lee De Forest was born on August 26, 1873 in *Council Bluffs, IA, the son of Henry Swift DeForest and Anna Robbins.* His father was a Congregational Church Minister and the President of Talladega College, an all-black school in Alabama. He had always hoped that his son would choose the same career path but De Forest had other plans De Forest completed his schooling from the Mount Hermon School and then enrolled at the Sheffield Scientific School at Yale University in Connecticut in 1893. Here he completed his graduation and earned his Ph.D. degree in 1899 with a dissertation on radio waves.

Contributions & Achievements:

After completing his graduation, he got employed at the Western Electric, where he *devised dynamos, telephone equipment,* and early *radio gear.* In 1902, he started his own business, the De Forest Wireless Telegraph Company, selling radio equipment and demonstrating the new technology by broadcasting Morse code signals. Within a span of four years, De Forest had been squeezed out of the management of his own company.

De Forest was highly creative and active, but many a times did not see the potential of his inventions or grasp their theoretical implications. While working on improving wireless telegraph equipment, he modified the vacuum tube invented by John Ambrose Fleming and designed the Audion (a vacuum tube containing some gas) in 1906. It was a *triode,* including a filament and a plate, like regular vacuum tubes, but also a grid between the filament and the plate. This reinforced the current through the tube, amplifying weak telegraph and even radio signals. De Forest thought the gas was an essential part of the system; however in 1912 others showed that a triode in a complete vacuum would function much better.

In 1913, the United States Attorney General sued De Forest for deceit on behalf of his shareholders, stating that his declaration of rebirth was an "absurd" promise (he was later acquitted). In 1916, the American inventor made two triumphs: the first radio advertisement (for his own products) and the first presidential election reported by radio.

In 1919, De Forest filed the first patent on his sound-on-film process, which enhanced the work of a Finnish inventor Eric Tigerstedt and the German partnership Tri-Ergon, and named it the *De Forest Phonofilm process*. This process involved recording sound directly onto film as parallel lines of variable shades of grey, and later became known as a 'variable density' system as opposed to 'variable area' systems, such as *RCA Photophone*.

Lee De Forest died in Hollywood on July 1, 1961, and was interred in San Fernando Mission Cemetery in Los Angeles, California. He died as a poor man with just $1,250 in his bank account at the time of his death.

Leland Clark

1918 - 2005

Leland C. Clark was born in 1918 in Rochester, New York. Known as the 'Father of Biosensors,' Dr. Clark invented the first device to rapidly determine the *amount of glucose in blood.* His sensor concept permits millions of *diabetics to monitor their own blood-sugar levels. He is most well-known as the inventor of the Clark electrode, a device used for measuring oxygen in blood, water and other liquids.*

Leland Clark started high school and discovered that science was an educational discipline, complete with course work, lab sessions and grades. He attended the Antioch College and the University of Rochester School Of Medicine, where he received his Ph.D. in biochemistry and physiology. Very soon, he became an assistant professor of biochemistry at Antioch and a research associate and chairman of the biochemistry department at a renowned institute. He also served as a professor of research pediatrics and head of the division of neurophysiology at the Children's Hospital Research Foundation for a long time.

Contributions & Achievements:

Now talking about his great inventions, he conducted a pioneering *research on heart-lung machines in the 1940s and 50s and was the holder of more than 25 patents. He is also the inventor of Oxycyte, a third-generation Per Fluorocarbon (PFC) therapeutic oxygen carrier designed to enhance oxygen delivery to damaged tissues.* Clark had studied the electrochemistry of oxygen gas reduction at platinum metal electrodes *In fact, Platinum electrodes used to detect oxygen electrochemically are often referred to generically as 'Clark electrodes'.*

More than almost any single invention, the *Clark Oxygen Electrode* has revolutionised the field of medicine for the past 50 years. *The Clark oxygen electrode remains the standard for measuring dissolved oxygen in environmental and industrial applications.*

Clark, one of the century's most prolific biomedical inventors and researchers, is also recognised for pioneering several medical milestones credited with saving thousands of lives and advancing the technology of modern medicine. His research accomplishments include the *development of the first successful heart-lung machine*, the advancement of technology leading to the development of one of the first intensive care units in the world, and pioneering research in biomedical applications of per fluorocarbons and biosensors.

Leland published more than *400 scientific papers in biomedicine* and generated numerous *US and foreign patents,* mainly *in the field of medical instrumentation and fluorocarbons.* He is the beneficiary of numerous honours and awards including induction into the National Academy of Engineering and the Engineering and Science Hall of Fame.

Leland Clark received the *American Physiological Society's Heyrovsky Award, in recognition of the invention of the membrane polarographic oxygen electrode.* He was a person who gave his all and was very dedicated to helping and using his talents to make a difference, to improve the quality of life for others. This great man died on September 25, 2005 at the age of 86.

Leonardo da Vinci

More commonly known as the greatest artist in the history of mankind, Leonardo da Vinci was also a magnificent philosopher and scientist. The most influential figure in the *Italian Renaissance, Leonardo* is widely considered to be an inventive multi-genius. Countless sketches describe that Leonardo had found out the basis for many inventions that were understood hundreds of years after his death.

Born in 1452 in Vinci, Italy, Leonardo was the illegitimate child of Ser Piero da Vinci, a notary, and Caterina, a country girl. He stayed with his father's family and they moved to Florence when he was just 12. At the tender age of 14, Leonardo started out his artist's apprenticeship at the studio of Andrea del Verrocchio (1435-1488), an Italian sculptor, goldsmith and painter. The young Leonardo earned a place into the painter's guild in 1472 when he was just 20 years old. At 26, he became an expert painter and owned a separate studio.

The art of painting made Leonardo knowledgable about anatomy and perspective. In addition to painting, Verrocchio's studio also offered technical and mechanical arts and sculpture. Leonardo had developed an interest in architecture so he went on to study engineering. His versatile and originative nature was born of a desire to promote creativity.

Contributions & Achievements:

After a decade of highly original work as an artist, Leonardo wrote to several wealthy men in 1482 to help finance his projects. The Duke of Milan, Lodovico Sforza (1452-1508), accepted his offer as Leonardo told him that he could design useful *war weapons like guns and mines,* and also *structures like collapsible bridges.* He lived in Milan with the Duke from 1482 to 1409, reportedly creating very *innovational war machines*. He also did painting and sculpture, as well as urban planning for large-scale water projects. His advice was sought for various projects related to architecture, military affairs and fortifications. There, he also wrote about making a *telescope to view the moon.*

Most of Leonardo's sketches and paintings depict a scientific phenomenon with an artistic and creative approach. On the other hand, his anatomical findings, including information about the structure of muscles and blood vessels, were surprisingly precise. His legendary masterpiece, *Mona Lisa (1503-1506), is said to have an unusual smile which depicts how the muscles of the face function to make a smile.* Leonardo also planned to create a *mechanical flying machine. Leonardo* discovered that flying, contrary to the popular notion, by attaching a pair of wings to a person's arms and then flapping them like a bird, is simply not possible. He concluded that by using levers, the wings of a flying structure could be controlled.

Leonardo also created a *sketch of an early helicopter* that even featured a *preventive parachute.* He, however, believed that his flying machines were not executable, partly because of his lack of knowledge about the bird flight. As *a result, he started studying animal anatomy, particularly of birds and bats.*

When France attacked Italy in 1944, Leonardo came back to Florence after the subsequent downfall of the Duke of Milan.

After his return, he became fully engaged in *mathematical studies.* Leonardo also accepted an invitation by the Duke of Valencia, Cesare Borgia (1475-1507), to work as a senior military architect and general engineer. During his tenure, he analysed geology and proposed to divert the Arno River and develop a canal that would allow Florence access to the sea.

Leonardo was approached by *King Francis I of France* (1494-1547) who gifted him a beautiful and peaceful castle near Amboise in the *Loire Valley*. This is the place where he completed some of his unfinished paintings. Some of his undeveloped ideas also include designs for a canal to link up two rivers that would have made a water route from the Atlantic Ocean to the Mediterranean Sea. Leonardo foresaw that the world would be swallowed up by massive floods in the years to come. His brilliant series of drawings display water in violent motion.

Leonardo da Vinci died at Amboise, Central France, on May 2, 1519. He was 67 years old.

Leonhard Euler

Leonhard Euler was an eminent Swiss mathematician and physicist, who is widely credited to be one of the founders of *pure mathematics.* He made significant contributions to *modern analytic geometry* and *trigonometry.* Euler's critical and formative work revolutionised the fields of *calculus, geometry* and *number theory.*

Leonhard Euler's father wished to see his son as a clergyman. He attended the University of Basel, where he soon developed an interest in geometry. Therefore, Euler, with support from his future teacher, Johann Bernoulli, persuaded his father to pursue mathematics.

Leonhard Euler became a member of the *St. Petersburg Academy of Science* in 1727. He also worked for Russian Navy from 1727 to 1730 as a medical lieutenant. At the academy, Euler served as professor of physics in 1730, and three years later, became a professor of mathematics in 1733.

Contributions & Achievements:

Euler published several articles during this time, and his book 'Mechanica' (1736-37), which was the first work to portray *Newtonian dynamics* in the form of mathematical analysis, earned him worldwide fame as a prominent mathematician. He joined the *Berlin Academy of Science in 1741* on the invitation of *Frederick the Great.* However, the two never got on well with each other. Nevertheless, Euler wrote more than *200 articles, three books* regarding *mathematical analysis* and a famous scientific publication, *'Letters to a Princess of Germany'* during his stay at Berlin.

Euler made groundbreaking contributions to analytical geometry, trigonometry, calculus and the number theory. He was the first person to integrate Leibniz's *differential calculus* and Newton's method of fluxions into mathematical analysis, and to state the *prime number theorem* and the law of *biquadratic reciprocity* when it came to the number theory. He published about *886 books* and *papers* and still remains the *most prolific writer of mathematics in history.*

Leonhard Euler died of a brain haemorrhage in 1783. He was 76 years old. Euler was buried next to his first wife, Katharina, at the Smolensk Lutheran Cemetery.

Linus Pauling

1901 – 1994

Linus Pauling was an American theoretical *physical chemist and activist.* He remains one of the greatest chemists ever, and the only person in history to be awarded *two unshared Nobel Prizes;* in 1954 for studying the nature of the chemical bond, and in 1962, for his efforts regarding the prohibition of nuclear testing. His contributions to *quantum chemistry* and *molecular biology* are considered revolutionary and created a universal impact.

Born in Portland, Oregon in 1901 to a pharmacist father, Linus Pauling acquired his undergraduate degree in chemical engineering from Oregon Agricultural College in Corvallis (now Oregon State University), where he also worked as a lecturer for about one year. Pauling received his Ph.D. from the California Institute of Technology in Pasadena, California. he took chemistry with minors in mathematics and physics.

Contributions & Achievements:

Linus Pauling travelled across Europe studying the *physics of atomic structure* at several universities. He also met many pioneers of atomic theory. Pauling soon developed an interest in examining the atomic structure of complex biological molecules by using *X-ray crystallography.*

Pauling accepted a teaching position at the California Institute of Technology, where he remained for the rest of his career. He analysed the chemical bond structure at the place. Pauling worked on the development of explosives, gas detectors and missiles for the US Navy during the World War II.

He later worked on examining the *chemical bonds that compose proteins.* The results he produced are still considered as the fundamental rules of biochemistry and have influenced several useful biotechnology applications. He was awarded the *1951 Nobel Prize in Chemistry* for his work on the determination of chemical bonds and its application related to the structure of biological molecules.

Pauling also received the *1962 Nobel Peace Prize* for his humanitarian efforts. He frequently brought out *controversial scientific theories.* He maintained moral positions regarding a few scientific issues.

Linus Pauling actively campaigned for social progress and humanitarian concerns, *such as public health and health promotion.* In the last few years of his life, he *furthered the health benefits of Vitamin C in combating diseases.* Pauling died in 1994 of prostate cancer in Big Sur, California.

Lise Meitner

Lise Meitner was an Austrian-born, later Swedish, physicist who shared the *Enrico Fermi Award in 1966,* with fellow chemists, *Otto Hahn* and *Fritz Strassmann,* for their collaborative work on the discovery of *uranium fission.* She remains one of the most important figures in the fields of *radioactivity and nuclear physics.*

The name of the chemical element, *meitnerium (Mt),* was suggested in Meitner's honour, who is also widely credited as the discoverer of *protactinium.*

Born into a prosperous Jewish family in Vienna, Lise Meitner's father was a prominent Jewish lawyer in Austria. She chose to convert to Christianity, being baptised in 1908.

Heavily motivated and influenced by her mentor, Ludwig Boltzmann, Meitner studied physics, becoming the second woman to earn a *doctoral degree in physics from the University of Vienna in 1905.*

After coming to Berlin for further education and research work, Lise Meitner started working on the new field of radioactivity with Otto Hahn. Her partnership and friendship with Hahn lasted a lifetime.

Meitner and Hahn discovered a new radioactive element, *protactinium, in 1918.* Meitner is probably best known for explaining, with another fellow physicist Otto Robert Frisch, some strange experimental results.

They had concluded that the nucleus had actually split in two halves, that later became known as the *process of fission.*

She did not share the Nobel Prize for this discovery which was simply absurd, because it was her discovery of fission that led to creation of the atomic bomb and to more peaceful uses of atomic energy.

Lise Meitner died on October 27, 1968 in Cambridge, England. She was 89 years old.

Louis de Broglie

1892 – 1987

Louis de Broglie (In full:Louis-Victor-Pierre-Raymond, 7e duc de Broglie) was an eminent French physicist. He gained worldwide acclaim for his groundbreaking work on *quantum theory.* In his 1924 thesis, he *discovered the wave nature of electrons* and suggested that all matter have *wave properties.* He won the *1929 Nobel Prize for Physics.*

Born in Dieppe, France in 1892, Louis de Broglie grew up in a rich, aristocratic family. He chose to study history after passing out of school in 1909. Broglie soon gained an interest in science and acquired a degree in physics in 1913. During the Wo rld War I, he was enlisted in the French Army. *He was posted in Eiffel Tower, where he had plenty of time to carry out experiments in radio communications and engineering.* After the war, Broglie started working with his brother, Maurice, in his lab.

Contributions & Achievements:

Most of the work in Maurice's lab involved X-rays, which made him think about the *dual nature of light;* more particularly, the wave–particle duality. Broglie soon suggested in his thesis for a doctorate degree that matter, also, might behave in a similar manner. When the French Academy became aware of his theory of electron waves, it caught Albert Einstein's attention, who had high praise for Broglie's bold ideas. That inspired the birth of *wave mechanics.*

Broglie's theory resolved and offered an explanation to a question that was brought up by calculations of the motion of electrons within the atom. It was later independently proved in 1927 by G.P. Thomson and Clinton Davisson and Lester Germer that matter actually could show wave-like characteristics. Louis de Broglie won the *1929 Nobel Prize in Physics* for his amazing work.

Broglie stayed at the Sorbonne after earning his doctorate, being appointed a professor of theoretical physics at the newly-established Henri Poincaré Institute in 1928, where he remained until his retirement in 1962.

Louis de Broglie acted as an adviser to the *French Atomic Energy Commissariat* after 1945. He won the Kalinga Prize by the UNESCO in 1952, and became a foreign member of the British Royal Society, as well as the French Academy of Sciences.

Broglie died on March 19, 1987 in Louveciennes, France. He was 94 years old.

Louis Pasteur

1822 - 1895

If one were to choose among the greatest supporters of humanity, Louis Pasteur would certainly rank at the top. *Louis Pasteur was a world renowned French chemist and biologist* born on December 27, 1822 in the town of Dole in Eastern France into the family of a poor tanner. Pasteur's work gave birth to many branches of science, and he was single Handedly responsible for some of the most important theoretical concepts and practical applications of modern science. Pasteur's Achievementss seem varied at first glance, but a more in-depth look at the evolution of his career specifies that there is a logical order to his discoveries.

He is respected for possessing the most important qualities of a scientist, the ability to survey all the known data and link, the data for all possible hypotheses, the patience and drive to conduct experiments under strictly controlled conditions, and the brilliance to uncover the road to the solution from the results.

The young Pasteur worked hard during his student days as he was not considered to be exceptional in any way at chemistry. He spent several years teaching and carrying out research at Dijon and Strasbourg and in 1854 moved to the University of Lille, where he became the professor of chemistry.

Contributions & Achievements:

When Pasteur started working as a chemist, he resolved a problem concerning the nature of tartaric acid (1849). Pasteur observed that the organic compound tartrate, when synthesized in a laboratory, was optically inactive (unable to rotate the plane of polarised light), unlike the tartrate from grapes, because the synthetic tartrate is composed of two optically asymmetric crystals. With cautious experimentation, he succeeded in separating the asymmetric crystals from each other and showed that each recovered optical activity. He then hypothesised that this molecular asymmetry is one of the mechanisms of life.

The mystery was that tartaric acid derived by chemical synthesis had no such effect, even though its chemical reactions were identical and its elemental composition was the same. In other words, living organisms only produce molecules that are of one specific orientation, and these molecules are always optically active. This was the first time anyone had demonstrated such a thing.

Pasteur founded the science of microbiology and proved that *most infectious diseases are caused by micro-organisms.* This became known as the *"germ theory" of disease.* The germ theory was the foundation of numerous applications, such as the large scale brewing of beer, wine-making and other antiseptic operations. Another significant discovery facilitated by the germ theory was the nature of contagious diseases. Pasteur's intuited that if germs were the cause of fermentation, they could just as well be the cause of contagious diseases. This proved to be true for many diseases, such as *potato blight, silkworm diseases,* and *anthrax.*

After studying the characteristics of germs and viruses that caused diseases, he and others found that laboratory manipulations of the infectious agents can be used to immunise people and animals. This treatment proved to work and saved countless lives and because of his study in germs, Pasteur encouraged many doctors to sanitise their hands and equipments before surgery.

Pasteur had a good *theoretical understanding of microbes.* He sought to apply his findings to the practical problem of stopping wine from spoiling. As many families depended on the wine industry for their livelihood, and the French economy was heavily dependent on wine exports, this was a big problem. Pasteur achieved success by slightly modifying the process used with the broth. Boiling the wine would alter its flavour. Therefore, Pasteur heated the wine enough to kill most of the microbes present without changing the flavour. Chilling prevented any microbes left from multiplying.

To his great delight, Pasteur found that this process could also prevent milks from turning sour and preserve many other foodstuffs as well. Thus, he became the inventor of a new process known as pasteurisation which brought him more fame and recognition. Besides this Pasteur also developed vaccines for several diseases including rabies. The discovery of the vaccine for rabies led to the founding of the *Pasteur Institute in Paris* in 1888.

On the discipline of rigid and strict experimental tests, he commented, "Imagination should give wings to our thoughts but we always need important experimental proof, and when the moment comes to draw conclusions and to understand the gathered observations, imagination must be checked and documented by the factual results of the experiment. All of these Achievementss point to singular brilliance and perseverance in Pasteur's nature. Pasteur's name lives on in the microbiological research institute in Paris that bears his name, the Institute Pasteur and continues to be today as a *Centre of Microbiology and Immunology.*

Lucretius

99 BC – 55 BC

Lucretius was a Roman poet and philosopher who wrote 'De rerum natura' (On the Nature of Things), an epic poem widely regarded as one of the most influential works in the history of literature, philosophy and science. In addition to his doctrinal and scientific impact, Lucretius extorted a profound influence on countless later philosophers and scientists.

Contributions & Achievements:

Very little is known about the life of Lucretius. He was born in 99 BC, according to most accounts. Jerome, a prominent Roman clergyman, wrote that a love potion had driven him insane. After writing some highly influential books in lucid intervals, Lucretius eventually committed suicide.

Probably one of the most influential works by Lucretius was his didactic poem, 'De rerum natura' (On the Nature of Things), that consisted of six volumes. He wrote about diverse things, such as atoms and the void, our modes of perception and our will.

He discussed the origin of the world and life, the causes of earthquakes, while reflecting on art, language, science and religion.

The poem also talked about a variety of diverse scientific topics, such as *cosmology, mental illness, nutrition, clouds, the seasons, eclipses magnet* and *poisoning.*

Lucretius was one of the first person to discover that everything in this *universe, ranging from planets and stars to mountains, decay.*

Centuries before the *second law of thermodynamics,* he predicted that one day, "the walls of the sky will be stormed on every side, and will collapse into a crumbling ruin … Nothing exists but acorns and the void." He rejected the idea of afterlife, and stated that the body was made up of atoms and governed by the *laws of nature.*

Lucretius died in 55 BC. He was around 44 years old.

Ludwig Boltzmann

Ludwig Boltzmann was an Austrian physicist whose efforts radically changed several branches of physics. He is mostly noted for his role in the development of *statistical mechanics* and the *statistical explanation of the second law of thermodynamics.*

Born in Vienna on February 20, 1844, Ludwig Boltzmann's father was a tax official. He earned his PhD degree in 1866 at the University of Vienna.

Ludwig Boltzmann taught mathematics, experimental physics and theoretical physics at several universities, but theoretical physics was his main passion. He wrote his famous travelogue "Reise eines deutschen Professors ins Eldorado" during this time.

Contributions & Achievements:

Boltzmann's scientific approach was to attack the problem. He explained the second law of thermodynamics in the early 1870s on the basis of the *atomic theory of matter.* He demonstrated that the second law could be interpreted by blending the laws of mechanics, applied to *the motions of the atoms, with the theory of probability.* He clarified that the second law is an essentially statistical law. He formulated most of the structure of statistical mechanics, which was later researched by the mathematical physicist Josiah Willard Gibbs.

In addition to his contributions to statistical mechanics, Boltzmann made detailed calculations in the kinetic theory of gases. He was probably the first person to understand the significance of James Clerk Maxwell's theory of electromagnetism, on which he wrote a two-volume treatise. Boltzmann also worked on a derivation for black-body radiation based on the Stefan's law, which was later termed by Hendrik Antoon Lorentz as 'a true pearl of theoretical physics'. His work in *statistical mechanics* was vocally criticised by Wilhelm Ostwald and the energeticists who disregarded atoms and based physical science exclusively on energy conditions. They were unable to understand the statistical nature of Boltzmann's logic.

His ideas were supported by the later discoveries in atomic physics in the early 1900, for instance the Brownian Motion, which can only be explained by *statistical mechanics.*

Ludwig Boltzmann was greatly demoralised due to the harsh criticisms of his works. He committed suicide on September 5, 1906 at Duino, Italy by hanging himself. He was 62 years old.

Luigi Galvani

Luigi Galvani was an Italian physician and physicist. One of the *early pioneers of bioelectricity,* he is known for his extraordinary work on the *nature and effects of electricity in an animal tissue,* which later led to *the invention of the voltaic pile.*

Born at Bologna, Italy, on September 9, 1737, Luigi Galvani, like his father, acquired a degree in medicine from Bologna's medical school.

Galvani took a job of comparative anatomist and gained fame for his research on the genitourinary tract of birds. In 1762, he became a lecturer of anatomy at the University of Bologna.

Contributions & Achievements:

During a random experiment on November 6, 1787, Galvani discovered that a frog muscle could be made to contract by placing an iron wire to the muscle and a copper wire to the nerve.

He built an instrument in which a frog's nerve was attached to an electrode of one metal, and an electrode of a different metal was attached with the frog muscle. He was well aware of the fact that an animal body grew convulsive movements when electricity was applied to it.

The discovery played a *historical role in bioelectricity,* as it proved *that electricity was not direct in its action.*

He established that it did not flow directly from the conductor into the frog muscle but was discharged from the conductor to another element in what he termed as a 'metallic arc'.

A few years later, Alessandro Volta's findings disputed his discovery and maintained that *animal electricity did not exist.*

While Galvani remained silent on the controversy, scholarly opinion was divided on the subject.

Finally, in 1843, Emil du Bois-Reymond successfully measured the injury potential from the frog muscle; therefore, putting an end to it.

Galvani died on December 4, 1798 in his childhood house in Bologna. He was 61 years old.

Lynn Margulis

1938 – 2011

Lynn Margulis was an eminent American biologist. Her serial *endosymbiotic theory* of *eukaryotic cell* development overturned the modern concept of how life originated on the earth. She also made vital contributions to the *Gaia theory,* which deals with the relation of living organisms to their inorganic surroundings.

Born in Chicago, Illinois in 1938, Lynn Margulis earned a bachelor's degree from the University of Chicago in 1957. After a few months, she married the famous astronomer, Carl Sagan.

They divorced in 1964. Margulis acquired a master's degree in zoology and genetics from the University of Wisconsin in 1960. She later earned a Ph.D. in genetics from the University of California, Berkeley in 1965.

Lynn Margolis is widely regarded as one of the most creative scientific theorists of the modern era.

Contributions & Achievements:

She formulated the symbiotic theory of evolution, which deals with the interconnection of prokaryotic and cukaryotic cells, explaining the emergence of new species by a mechanism known as 'symbiogenesis'.

In 1983, she was elected to the *National Academy of Sciences.* She was awarded the the *Darwin-Wallace Medal of the Linnean Society of London in 2008.*

Her contemporaries either describe her as revolutionary or as an eccentric person. Famous sociobiologist E. 0. Wilson has honoured her as the 'most successful synthetic thinker of modern biology'.

Science, the prestigious academic journal, has identified her as

'Science's unruly Earth mother.'

Lynn Margulis died of a *hemorrhagic stroke* on November 22, 2011. She was 73 years old.

Marcello Malpighi

Marcello Malpighi was an eminent Italian physician and biologist. Widely regarded as one of the founders of microscopic anatomy, he made crucial contributions in the fields of *physiology, practical medicine* and *embryology*.

Born on March 10, 1628 in a rich family of Crevalcore, Italy, Marcello Malpighi started attending the *University of Bologna* when he was only 17. He received doctorates in both medicine and philosophy in 1653.

Contributions & Achievements:

Marcello Malpighi was one of the first scientists to use the *newly invented microscope* for studying *tiny biological entities.* He analysed several parts of the organs of bats, frogs and other animals under the microscope. Malpighi, while studying the structure of lungs, noticed its membranous alveoli and the hair-like connections between veins and arteries, which he named them as *capillaries*. The discovery established how the oxygen we breathe enters the blood stream and serves the body. He was also the first person to study red blood corpuscles and the mucous layer under the epidermis.

Malpighi gained worldwide acclaim when the *Royal Society* published his findings. Malpighi's study of the life cycle of plants and animals were quite influential to the subject of reproduction. He extensively studied the *transformation of caterpillars into insects, chick embryo development* and seed development in plants.

Malpighi is also considered to be the founder of *modern anatomy.*

His contributions were very important and groundbreaking.

Marcello Malpighi was appointed a *Papal physician in Rome, Italy* by Pope Innocent XII in 1691. Only three years later, he died of apoplexy on November 30, 1694. Malpighi was 66 years old.

Maria Goeppert-Mayer

1906 - 1972

The German physicist and mathematician, Maria Goeppert-Mayer is prominent for her numerous contributions to the field of physics which earned her a *Nobel Prize* in Physics in 1963. *She was the first woman to win the Nobel Prize for theoretical physics and the second woman in history to win a Nobel Prize— the first being Marie Curie. She is most famous for proposing the nuclear shell model of the atomic nucleus.*

Maria Goeppert Mayer was born on June 28, 1906, Kattowitz, Germany (now Katowice, Poland). She was the only child of Friedrich Goeppert, a progressive professor of Pediatrics at the University at Göttingen and Maria nee Wolff, a former music teacher. When she was very young her family moved to Göttingen in 1910, where Maria was educated at a *girls' grammar school* operated by suffragettes. The school went bankrupt after her junior year, but she passed a collegiate examination without a high school diploma and earned her PhD under Max Born at the University of Göttingen in 1930. The same year she married Dr. Joseph Edward Mayer, an assistant of James Franck. After marriage they both moved to the United States.

Contributions & Achievements:

Women during that time were generally regarded unsuitable in the upper realms of academia, and despite her doctorate for years she was largely limited to unpaid and unofficial work in university laboratories, her presence only accepted because of her husband. In the following few years, Goeppert-Mayer worked at unofficial or volunteer positions, initially at the Johns Hopkins University in Baltimore, Maryland, from 1931–39, the then Columbia University in 1940-46, and after that the University of Chicago. Later, she also took different positions that came her way: a teaching position at the Sarah Lawrence College, a research position with the Columbia University's Substitute Alloy Materials Project and with the Opacity Project. She also spent some time at the Los Alamos Laboratory.

During her husband's time at the University of Chicago, Goeppert-Mayer volunteered to become an Associate Professor of Physics at the school. Within a few months of her arrival, when the nearby Argonne National Laboratory was founded on July 1, 1946, Goeppert-Mayer was offered a part-time job there as a Senior Physicist in the Theoretical Physics Division. This was the first time in her career that she was working and paid at a level commensurate with her training and expertise. Two years later, she made the breakthrough that earned her tremendous fame and respect in her field.

During 1960, Goeppert-Mayer was appointed to a position as a (full) Professor of Physics at the University of California at San Diego.

Development of the Structure of Nuclear Shells:

It was during her time at Chicago and Argonne that she developed a *mathematical model* for the structure of nuclear shells. With Edward Teller (one of her colleagues at Argonne National Laboratory), she conducted inquiries about the source of the elements, and noticed the repetition of seven 'magic numbers', as she named them — 2, 8, 20, 28, 50, 82, and 126. Elements with a 'magic number' of protons or neutrons were consistently more stable than elements with other numbers of protons or neutrons. On the basis of this, she proposed in that inside the nucleus, protons and neutrons are arranged in a series of nucleon layers, like the layers of an onion, with neutrons and protons rotating around each other at each level. During the same time but working independently, German physicist J. Hans D. Jensen reached the same conclusion.

Goeppert-Mayer was awarded the *Nobel Prize in Physics in 1963,* shared with J. Hans D. Jensen and Eugene Paul Wigner for their proposal of the *Shell Nuclear Model.*

Goeppert-Mayer died due to a heart failure in San Diego, California, on February 20, 1972.

Marie Curie

The famous chemist and physicist, Marie Curie was the first person in the history to be awarded with the *two Nobel Prizes* in diverse fields of *science (chemistry and physics). She is notable for her theory of radioactivity, techniques for isolating radioactive isotopes and the discovery of two new elements, polonium and radium. Her work has received great appreciation from many scientists all over the world.*

Marie Curie was born in Warsaw on November 7, 1867. She was the fifth and the youngest daughter of a secondary-school teacher. Her early years were very difficult with her mother and her sister passing away. She received her early education from some local school and her father taught her mathematics and physics, subjects that Marie was to pursue. She lived in Warsaw until she was twenty-four years old and later moved to Paris to receive higher education at the Sorbonne. There she obtained Licenciateships in Physics and the Mathematical Sciences.

In 1894, she met Pierre Curie, instructor in the School of Physics and Chemistry. Marie had begun her scientific career in Paris with an examination of the magnetic properties of various steels; it was their common interest in magnetism that brought Marie and Pierre together. The following year they got married.

Contributions & Achievements:

In 1896, when Henry Becquerel made his discovery of radioactivity, the Curie's became inspired to look into uranium rays as a possible field of research for a thesis. In 1898, their brilliant researches led to the discovery of polonium, named after the country of Marie's birth, and radium. In 1903, the *Royal Swedish Academy of Sciences* honoured both *Pierre Curie and Marie Curie* with the *Nobel Prize* in Physics, for their joint researches on the *radiation phenomena* discovered by *Becquerel.*

Following the unfortunate death of her husband in 1906, she took his place as *Professor of General* Physics in the *Faculty of Sciences.* She was the first woman who had held this position. She was also employed as *Director at the Curie Laboratory in the Radium Institute of the University of Paris*, founded in 1914.

After her husband's death, she continued with her efforts of developing methods for obtaining pure radium from radioactive residues in sufficient quantities. *By 1910, she successfully isolated the pure radium metal.*

In 1911, Curie was awarded with yet another Nobel Prize, this time in Chemistry in recognition of her work in radioactivity.

All her life Marie promoted the use of radium and also set a great example of its use during the World War I for healing the injuries of those who suffered. Her passion for science is reflected in all her efforts towards its advancement. She was also a member of the *Conseil du Physique, Solvay* from 1911 until her death. Moreover, since 1922, she had been a member of the Committee of Intellectual Co-operation of the League of Nations. In 1932, she also laid the foundation of Radium Institute (now the Maria Skodowska–Curie Institute of Oncology) in Warsaw. Her work is recorded in various papers and in scientific journals.

Death

The great scientist Marie Curie died on July 4, 1934 at the Sancellemoz Sanatorium in Passy, in Haute-Savoie from aplastic anemia.

Her name will always be written in golden letters for her tremendous contributions in the field of science.

Max Born

1882 – 1970

Max Born was a German physicist who played a vital role in the evolution of *quantum mechanics.* His theoretical work in *solid-state physics* and *optics* is also considered very influential. Born shared the *1954 Nobel Prize for Physics* with *Walther Bothe* for his statistical interpretation of quantum theory.

Born in 1882 in Breslau, German Empire, Max Born's father was an anatomist and embryologist. He recieved his early education from the König-Wilhelm-Gymnasium. He attended the University of Breslau, and later the Heidelberg University and the University of Zurich. Born earned his doctorate at the University of Göttingen in 1907, under the supervision of famous mathematician Felix Klein.

Contributions & Achievements:

Max Born was a highly successful theoretical physicist who made brilliant contributions in the areas of *physics and optics.* He was appointed the Professor of Theoretical Physics at the University of Göttingen in 1921, where he established an *authoritative school for atomic and quantum physics.*

Born also worked with Werner Heisenberg for a while and discovered the 'arrays of numbers' that could be employed to prepare the first in-depth quantum theory. Born was more proficient in mathematics than Heisenberg and he found out that these 'arrays' were widely known in mathematics as *matrices*. Around 1926, Born and his assistant formulated a full explanation of the new theory.

Perhaps, Born's most influential contribution to the *quantum theory* was his concept that the wave-function could only be employed to predict the probabilities of different results being concluded in measurements; more precisely, that the square of the wave-function symbolises a probability density. The concept was termed as the *statistical interpretation of quantum theory.*

Max Born was very disappointed not to share the 1932 Nobel Prize for Physics with Heisenberg. Making things worse, he was forced to leave Göttingen as a *Jew* after the rise of *Adolf Hitler.* He spent three years in Cambridge, and alter became a Professor of Natural Philosophy in the University of Edinburgh, where he stayed until 1953. After his retirement, Born returned to Germany. Finally in 1954, he was awarded Nobel Prize in the Physics for the statistical interpretation of quantum theory, sharing with his fellow nuclear physicist, *Walther Bothe.*

Born died on January 5, 1970 in Göttingen, Germany. He was 87 years old.

Max Planck

1858 – 1947

Max Karl Ernst Ludwig Planck was born in Kiel, Germany, on April 23, 1858, This German Physicist made many great contributions to theoretical physics, but his fame rests primarily on his role as the *originator of the quantum theory.* This theory revolutionised our understanding of atomic and sub-atomic processes, just as Albert Einstein's Theory of Relativity revolutionized our understanding of space and Time. Together they constitute the fundamental theories of the 20th-century. Planck was also awarded the *Nobel Prize in Physics in 1918.*

Planck was born in a large family and was brought up in a tradition which greatly respected scholarship, honesty, fairness and generosity. The values he was given as a young child quickly became the values that he would cherish throughout his life, showing the utmost respect for the institutions of the state and church. Max began his elementary schooling in Kiel. He did well at school but not brilliantly, usually coming somewhere between third and eighth in his class. Music was perhaps his best subject and he was awarded the *school prize in catechism* and *good conduct almost every year.* However, towards the end of his school career, his teachers raised his level of interest in *physics and mathematics,* and he became deeply impressed by the absolute nature of the *law of conservation of energy*. Planck describes why he chose physics:

Contributions & Achievements:

"The outside world is something independent from man, something absolute, and the quest for the laws which apply to this absolute appeared to me as the most sublime scientific pursuit in life."

Planck was appointed the *professor of theoretical physics* at the University of Berlin. While in Berlin, Planck did his most luminous work and delivered outstanding lectures. He studied thermodynamics in particular examining the distribution of energy according to the wavelength. By combining the formulae of Wien and Rayleigh, Planck announced a new formula now known as '*Planck's radiation formula.*' Within two months the Planck made a complete theoretical deduction of his formula giving up classical physics and introducing the *quanta of energy.* On December 14, 1900, he presented his theoretical explanation involving the quanta of energy at a meeting of the Physikalische Gesellschaft in Berlin. He announced his derivation of the relationship which was based on the revolutionary idea that the energy emitted by a resonator could only take on discrete values or quanta. The energy for a resonator of frequency v is hv, where h is a *universal constant,* now called *Planck's constant.*

The discovery of Planck's constant enabled him to define a new universal set of physical units (such as the Planck length and the Planck mass), all based on fundamental physical constants. Planck's work on the quantum theory, as it came to be known, was published in the Annalen der Physik. His work is summarised in two books Thermodynamik (Thermodynamics) and Theorie der Wärmestrahlung (Theory of heat radiation).

This was not only Planck's most important work but also marked a turning point in the history of physics. The importance of the discovery, with its far-reaching effect on classical physics, was not appreciated at first. However, the evidence for its validity gradually became irresistible as its application accounted for many differences between the observed phenomena and the classical theory.

Planck was also a *philosopher of science.* In his Scientific Autobiography and Other Papers, he stated Planck's Principle, which holds that 'A new scientific truth does not triumph by convincing its opponents and making them see the light, but rather because its opponents eventually die and a new generation grows up, that is familiar with it'.

This great man died on October 4, 1947 at the age of 89 in Gottingen, West Germany.

Max von Laue

Max von Laue was a German physicist, who, won the *1914 Nobel Prize in physics* for his discovery of *X-ray crystallography,* which helps in determining the arrangement of atoms in some substances.

Born in Pfaffendorf, Sachsen, Germany in 1879, Max von Laue studied physics at the University of Strasbourg, and later, the Universities of Göttingen and Munich. He received his Ph.D. in physics from the University of Berlin in 1903.

Max von Laue worked as an *assistant to his mentor, Max Planck*, at the *Institute for Physics in Berlin*. He was appointed the *deputy director* to *Albert Einstein* at the *Institute for Physics in 1917.*

Contributions & Achievements:

Laue's initial interests were in *optics* and the *wave theory of light.* When Wilhelm Röntgen discovered X-rays in 1895, scientists were not sure if they were particles or short electromagnetic waves. Laue predicted in 1912 that X-rays could be diffracted by a crystal acting, as a *natural diffraction grating.* Later experiments with several crystals produced patterns, which were termed as *Laue patterns*, from which the crystal structure could be interpreted.

Einstein praised Laue's work as one of the most beautiful discoveries in physics. His contributions gave birth to the *X-ray spectroscopy,* the exploration of atomic structures of chemical elements and the determination of *X-ray wavelength. X-ray structural analysis played a vital role in modern physics and chemistry, with practical applications in various industries.*

In his later years, Max von Laue worked on the forces between atoms and also studied the *Thermodynamics of Superconductivity*. He wrote several famous books on the history of physics and Einstein's *Theory of Relativity*. During World War II, Laue was arrested by the Allied forces and, like other German scientists, was sent to England. He came back to Germany in 1946 and took charge of the *Max Planck Institute,* Göttingen.

He was appointed the director of the Fritz Haber Institute, Berlin in 1951, when he was 71 years old. Laue retired seven years later in 1958.

Max von Laue died on April 24, 1960. He was 80 years old.

Michael Faraday

1791-1867

English scientist and physicist, Michael Faraday is known for his brilliant discoveries of *electro-magnetic induction, electro-magnetic rotations, the magneto-optical effect, diamagnetism, field theory* and much more. Many famous historians regard him as the most influential and exemplary experimentalist in the history of science. The incredible scope and profundity of Faraday's work spanned a time of 60 years. He is considered as one of the top figures of the 19th century for his remarkable contribution in the *field of electricity.*

This British scientist was born in Newington Butts, London on September 22, 1791. Faraday was born as the third-child in a poor family, where his father, James was a blacksmith. Due to the poor family background, young Faraday could not enjoy the niceties of a big school and had to largely educate himself. He developed a great love for reading after he became apprenticed to a local bookbinder and bookseller George Riebau. After studying the work of great scientists and authors, he developed an interest in science, particularly in electricity. It was his early reading and experiments with the idea of force, that enabled him to make imperative discoveries in electricity later in life.

Contributions & Achievements:

Faraday was always extremely curious and inquisitive. After the end of his apprenticeship (at the age of twenty), he began to attend lectures of different famous chemists in the quest to learn more. During this time, he also applied for a job to Humphry Davy, his chemistry lecturer who later appointed him as Chemical Assistant at the Royal Institution in 1813. Few years later in 1821, Faraday married Sarah Barnard whom he met at the Sandemanian church.

After Davy retired in 1827, Faraday replaced him as lecturer of chemistry at the Royal Institution and published all his research work related to condensation of gases, optical deceptions and the isolation of benzene from gas oils.

During the time when he was hired as an assistant to Professor Davy, Faraday discovered two new chlorides of carbon, conducted experiments on the diffusion of gases, investigated the alloys of steel, and produced several new kinds of glass intended for optical purposes.

Faraday is best recognised for his contributions to *electricity* and *magnetism*. In 1821, after being inspired by the work of Danish physicist and chemist, Hans Christian, he began experimenting with *electromagnetism* and by signifying the conversion of electrical energy into motive force, devised the *electric motor.* For the next few years he continued conducting experiments from his initial electromagnetic discovery. In 1831, Faraday discovered the induction of electric currents and constructed the first *electric dynamo*. In 1839, he conducted several experiments to determine the fundamental nature of electricity and established that electrostatic force consists of a field of curved lines of force and conceived a specific inductive capacity. This led to the development of his theories on light and gravitational systems. His other prominent discoveries include: the *process of diamagnetism,* the *Faraday Effect, Faraday cage* and many more.

Two of his famous books are the 'Experimental Researches in Electricity' and the 'Chemical History of the Candle.'

During the later years of his life, he made several other Achievementss: received a Doctor of Civil Law degree in 1832 by the University of Oxford and was, elected as a foreign member of the Royal Swedish Academy of Sciences in 1838 and the French Academy of Sciences in 1844.

For his great contributions to science, the British government granted him a pension and a house in Hampton Court, where he spent the rest of his life after his retirement in 1858.

The great British scientist departed from this world on August 25, 1867.

Michio Kaku

Most well known in the world of theoretical physicists, Michio Kaku is a professor of the City College of New York. He is considered as a futurist, a great communicator, and a modern popularizer of science. He is the author of several physics-related books, such as the *Physics of the Impossible* published in 2008, and *Physics of the Future* published in 2011. Michio Kaku has appeared in several television programs, radio programs, films and makes his work available through his online blogs.

Michio Kaku was born in January 24, 1947 to Japanese parents who have Tibetan ancestry. His grandfather immigrated to the United States to help with the 1906 cleanup operation for the San Francisco Earthquake. He was born in San Jose, California. Around the time of the Vietnam War, he was able to complete the basic training given by the U.S. Army at Fort Benning and he even had his Infantry training in Washington. Before he was even deployed as an infantryman, however, the war had already ended.

He has shown a great interest in science ever since he was young. When he studied in Palo Alto's Cubberley High School, he assembled his own particle accelerator inside the garage of his parents. According to him, his goal was to generate *gamma ray beams* that would be strong enough to be able to produce anti-matter. In Albuquerque, New Mexico, he attended the *National Science Fair* and it was there where he had the attention of Edward Teller, a physicist who took him as his protégé. He then earned the *Hertz Engineering Scholarship.*

Michio Kaku was first in his physics class and in 1968, he graduated summa cum laude at Harvard University. In Berkeley, at the University of California, he received his Ph.D. in 1972 after attending the Berkeley

Radiation Laboratory. In that same year, he had a lectureship at none other than the Princeton University.

This modern day man of science is knowledgeable in several fields, such as hadronic physics, supersymmetry, supergravity, superstring theory, and quantum physics among others. His knowledge on these topics has been subject of more than 70 publications in different journals covering physics-related subjects, such as *Physics Review.*

Contributions & Achievements:

Michio Kaku is known as a popularizer of science, and he has authored several popular science textbooks. His first book was released in 1994 – *Hyperspace*, followed by "Beyond Einstein" which he wrote with Jennifer Thompson a year later. In 1998, he published "Visions: How Science Will Revolutionize the 21st Century." It took a while before he published "Einstein's Cosmos" and "Parallel Worlds" in 2004. His most recent works are "Physics of the Impossible" published in 2008 and "Physics of the Future" published in 2011.

All of these publications spark a great interest in the minds of individuals, both scholars and curious minds alike who are interested in the realm of theoretical physics and other related disciplines given the futurist vision that Michio Kaku believes in.

Michio Kaku's publications reflect his involvement in the ongoing search of understanding and unifying the forces of nature into just one theory. He continues his works based on Einstein's earlier findings, and Michio Kaku is known as one of the founders of string field theory. His book Hyperspace was a great best seller and was voted as one of the top science books by both The Washington Post and The New York Times in the same year.

The Populariser of Science

This is a commonly heard phrase whenever Michio Kaku's name is mentioned, and not without good reason. Apart from comprehensive publications of both books and journal articles, he has a known presence in many different forms of media.

He has made appearances on several television channels—notable ones such as BBC, Discovery, ABC, CNN, and the Science Channel just to name a few. Apart from his publications in Physics Review, his works and articles are also available to the public through science publications such as Wired, New Scientist, and Discover.

Some of his more recent media exposure includes BBC's series on

Time where he went through an extraordinary exploration in search of time, Vision of the Future of BBC Four series where he explored today's science as well as that of the future and beyond, and The Universe of the History Channel.

On a weekly basis, Michio Kaku can be heard on radio programs which are broadcasted all over the country. He hosts Science Fantastic and Explorations in Science. Apart from these weekly radio programs, his talks about physics and his studies can be seen in several websites dedicated to his work, and even on YouTube channels. He has also been part of documentaries such as Obsessed and Scientific which discusses the possibility of time travel, UFOs: Seeing is Believing of ABC, and he was one of the scientists who were featured in "Me and Isaac Newton." For BBC, he has hosted the three-hour documentary called Visions of the Future. There was even a period in his career back in 2009 when he hosted a weekly TV series for 12 episodes at the Science Channel called Sci Fi Science: Physics of the Impossible. One of his more interesting thoughts has been featured on Discovery Channel's Alien Planet where he discussed the possible future of interstellar exploration.

It is because of his presence through different media and his skill when it comes to communicating the otherwise complex theories into information which is easier to understand that has earned him the name popularizer of science. In his videos, he is able to convey the messages and central thoughts of theories without making it hard for his audience to understand, but enough to get them hooked on the science behind different matters.

Despite his amazing academic endeavors and several appearances, he is a father to two daughters and is married to Shizue Kaku. His favourite songs include the Star Wars Theme as well as Star Trek's The Next Generation Theme, both in line with his interest in physics and interstellar matters of science.

Mohammad Abdus Salam

1926– 1996

Mohammad Abdus Salam, was born in January 29, 1926 in Punjab. He was a *Pakistani theoretical physicist* and a renowned, astrophysicist. He was also the first Pakistani and Muslim (he belonged to Ahmadiyya Muslim Community) to win the *Nobel laureate in Physics* for his work in *Electro-Weak Theory.*

Contributions & Achievements:

Salam, Sheldon Glashow and Steven Weinberg shared the prize for this discovery. He received the *Smith's Prize* from the Cambridge University, for the pre-doctoral contribution to Physics and the *Hopkins Prize.* Later on, he wrote a doctoral thesis on the fundamental work in *Quantum electrodynamics.* This was published in 1951 and enabled him to earn the *Adams Prize.* In 1956, he was invited to take a chair at the Imperial College, London, where he and Paul Matthews created a lively theoretical physics group. During the early 1960s, however, Salam played a very significant role in establishing the Pakistan Atomic Energy Commission (PAEC) – the atomic research agency of Pakistan – and Space and Upper Atmosphere Research Commission (SUPARCO) – the Space Research Agency of Pakistan, of which he was the founding director.

He was also the founder of the Third World Academy of Sciences (TWAS)and the International Center for Theoretical Physics (ICTP) .

Salam was also responsible for initiating research on water logging and salinity problems in Pakistan. He also played a critical role in agricultural research, PAEC and SUPARCO, the international space agency in Pakistan. Abdus Salam was the pioneer of all the important developments in the theoretical elementary particle physics. He also served on a number of United Nations committees, concerning science and technology in developing countries. Abdus Salam prepared and taught future Pakistani engineers and scientists in the field of mathematics and physics.

His contributions was research on the physics of elementary particles. His most famous contributions included: Two-component neutrino theory and the prediction of the inevitable parity violation in weak interaction, gauge unification of weak and *electromagnetic interaction.* This unified force is known as the 'Electroweak' force, a name given to it by Salam, and which lays the foundation of the *Standard Model* in particle physics and predicted the existence of weak neutral currents and W particles and Z particles before their experimental discovery, symmetry properties of elementary particles; unitary symmetry, renormalization of meson theories, gravity theory and its role in particle physics; two tensor theory of gravity and strong interaction physics, unification of electroweak with strong nuclear forces, grand unification theory, related prediction of proton-decay.

Some other contributions of Salam include the *Pati-Salam model,* a grand unification Theory, Super Symmetry Theory, in particular, formulation of Super Space and Formalism of Super Fields in 1974, the theory of super manifolds, as a Geometrical framework for understanding super symmetry, in 1974, Super geometry, the geometric basis for super symmetry, in 1974, the application of the Higgs Mechanism to the electroweak symmetry breaking and prediction of the magnetic photon in 1966.

Abdus Salam died on November 21, 1996 at the age of 70 in Oxford, England after a prolonged illness. His body was brought to Pakistan and buried in the *Bahishti Maqbara* in *Rabwah.* His memory will live on forever in the hearts of Pakistanis' as he showed the world the true potential of a Pakistani.

Muhammad ibn Musa al-Khwarizmi

780 - 850

Muhammad ibn Musa al-Khwarizmi was a Persian mathematician, astronomer, astrologer geographer and a scholar in the House of Wisdom in Baghdad. He was born in Persia of that time around 780. Al-Khwarizmi was one of the learned men who worked in the *House of Wisdom*. Al-Khwarizmi flourished while working as a member of the House of Wisdom in Baghdad under the leadership of Kalif al-Mamun, the son of the Khalif Harun al-Rashid, who was made famous in the *Arabian Nights*. The House of Wisdom was a scientific research and teaching centre.

Al-Khwarizmi developed the concept of the algorithm in mathematics (which is a reason for his being called the *grandfather of computer science* by some people).]

Contributions & Achievements:

Al-Khwarizmi's algebra is regarded as the foundation and cornerstone of the sciences. To al-Khwarizmi, we owe the world 'algebra,' from the title of his greatest mathematical work, Hisab al-Jabr wa-al-Muqabala. The book, which was twice translated into Latin, by both Gerard of Cremona and Robert of Chester in the 12th century, works out several hundred simple quadratic equations by analysis as well as by geometrical example. It also has substantial sections on methods of dividing up inheritances and surveying plots of land. It is largely concerned with methods for solving practical computational problems rather than algebra as the term is now understood.

Al-Khwarizmi confined his discussions to equations of the first and second degrees. He also wrote an important work on astronomy, covering calendars, calculating true positions of the sun, moon and planets, tables of sines and tangents, spherical astronomy, astrological tables, parallax and eclipse calculations, and visibility of the moon. His astronomical work, Zij al-sindhind, is also based on the work of other scientists. As with the Algebra, its chief interest is as the earliest Arab work still in existence in Arabic.

His most recognised work as mentioned above and one that is so named after him is the mathematical concept, *Algorithm*. The modern meaning of the word relates to a specific practice for solving a particular problem. Today, people use algorithms to do additions and long divisions, principles that are found in Al-Khwarizmi's text written over 2000 years ago. Al-Khwarizmi was also responsible for introducing the Arabic numbers to the West, setting in motion a process that led to the use of the nine Arabic numerals, together with the zero sign.

Of great importance also was al-Khwarizmi's contribution to medieval geography. He systematised and corrected Ptolemy's research in geography, using his own original findings that are entitled as Surat al-Ard (The Shape of the Earth). The text exists in a manuscript; the maps have unfortunately not been preserved, although modern scholars have been able to reconstruct them from al-Khwarizmi's descriptions. He supervised the work of 70 geographers to create a map of the then "known world". When his work became known in Europe through Latin translations, his influence made a permanent mark on the development of science in the West.

Al-Khwarizmi made several important improvements to the theory and construction of sundials, which he inherited from his Indian and Hellenistic predecessors. He made tables for these instruments which considerably shortened the time needed to make specific calculations. His sundial was universal and could be observed from anywhere on the Earth. From then on, sundials were frequently placed on mosques to determine the time of prayer. The shadow square, an instrument used to determine the linear height of an object, in conjunction with the alidade for angular observations, was also invented by al-Khwarizmi in ninth-century Baghdad.

While his major contributions were the result of original research, he also did much to synthesise the existing knowledge in these fields from Greek, Indian, and other sources. A number of minor works were written by al-Khwarizmi on topics such as the astrolabe, on which he wrote on the Jewish calendar. He also wrote a political history containing horoscopes of prominent persons.

Muhammad ibn Musa al-Khwarizmi died in c. 850 being remembered as one of the most seminal scientific minds of the early Islamic culture.

Murray Gell-Mann

Murray Gell-Mann is an American physicist who is credited with the introduction of the *concept of quarks.* He won the *1969 Nobel Prize for physics* for his groundbreaking work on the description and classification of sub-atomic particles. Gell-Mann is widely considered to be one of the greatest and the most influential physicists of the 20th century.

Borin in 1929 in Manhattan, New York City, Murray Gell-Mann was a very gifted student who entered the Yale University when he was only 15. He acquired a B.S. degree in physics in 1948, and earned his *Ph.D.* at the *Massachusetts Institute of Technology* in 1951.

His doctoral thesis on sub-atomic particles greatly inspired the works of Hungarian American theoretical physicist and Nobel laureate Eugene Wigner.

Murray Gell-Mann started working at the Institute for Nuclear Studies, University of Chicago in 1952, where he introduced the concept of *'strangeness', a quantum property and the force that holds the components of the atomic nucleus, in 1953.*

He became a member of the faculty of the California Institute of Technology, Pasadena in 1955, and the Robert Andrews Millikan Professor of Theoretical Physics in 1967.

Contributions & Achievements:

While working with fellow physicist Yuval Ne'eman, in 1961, Gell-Mann suggested a scheme for the classification of previously discovered strongly interacting particles into a basic and proper arrangement of families.

He hypothesised that it should be achievable to elaborate on the specific properties of known particles in terms of even more fundamental particles. He later termed these basic particles of matter as 'quarks', which later led to the *1964 discovery of the omega-minus particle.*

Murray Gell-Mann served as a *director of the MacArthur Foundation for 23 years, from 1979 to 2002.* He was also a member of the President's Committee of Advisors on Science and Technology from 1994 to 2001.

Nicolaus Copernicus

Also known as the founder of modern astronomy, Nicolaus Copernicus was the first person to devise a comprehensive *heliocentric cosmology,* which displaced the Earth from the centre of the universe. Copernicus' *heliocentric theory* acted as the *catalyst for the scientific revolution of the 16th and 17th centuries,* which is sometimes known as the *Copernican revolution.* His work forever changed the place of man in the cosmos; no longer could man legitimately think his importance greater than his fellow creatures. Besides an astronomer, he was also a great mathematician, physician, quadrilingual polyglot, classical scholar, translator and artist.

Nicolaus Copernicus was born on February 19, 1473 in the city of Toru (Thorn) in Royal Prussia, where his father, a native of Krakow, had established as a wholesale merchant. His mother was the daughter of a wealthy Toru merchant. Nicolaus was the youngest child in the family. After his father's death, he was raised by his mother's brother, Lucas Watzelrode, a bishop in the Catholic Church. In 1941-1942 Nicolaus completed his matriculation from Kraków Academy after which he devoted himself, during three years, to mathematical science under Albert Brudzewski and incidentally attained some painting skills.

During his time at the Kraków Academy he acquired a thorough mathematical-astronomical knowledge. He also studied the idealistic and natural-science writings of Aristotle and Averroes that stirred his interest in learning, and made him familiar with humanistic culture. In 1497 he resumed his studies, this time in Italy, where he went to many universities including Bologna, Padua and Ferrara. There he completed his bi-doctorate in medicine and law. By attending astronomical lectures of many Italian astronomers such as Domenico Maria Novara, Copernicus extended his astronomical knowledge.

After studying for six years, Copernicus returned to Poland in the year 1503, where he was appointed as a canon in the cathedral of Frauenburg and spent a protected life for the rest of his days. In addition to his clerical duties, he continued his astronomical research and medical practice.

Contributions & Achievements:

From 1513, the foundation of his great work was laid down at Frauenburg, where he began work on his *heliocentric theory.* His theory was a concise description of the world's heliocentric mechanism, without mathematical apparatus, and varyied in some important aspects of geometric construction from De revolutionibus; but it was already based on the same assumptions regarding Earth's triple motions.

He wrote a manuscript explaining his new theory which was read by many astronomers, and rumours of Copernicus' claim that the earth revolves about the sun spread all through Europe. His theory attracted many mathematicians and various astronomers who came to Copernicus to learn more about his new theory. One of them, Rheticus, even published a book unfolding this theory in 1540. Even though Copernicus finished writing his book, *De revolutionibus orbium coelestium,* about a decade earlier, in 1530, he postponed its publication fearing the reactions his ground-breaking theory might stir up.

However, he finally published his book in 1543, the same year he died. His book is considered to serve the beginning of modern astronomy and the defining epiphany that began the scientific revolution.

Niels Bohr

1885 - 1962

Niels Henrik David Bohr is considered as one of most dominant and influential physicists of the 20th century. His remarkable work in understanding the *Atomic Structure and Quantum Mechanics* earned him the *Nobel Price in Physics in 1922.* He also acted as a prominent part of the team of physicists working on the *Manhattan Project.* His contributions to the field of physics has received remarkable praise from many scientists all over the world.

The Danish physicist was born on October 7, 1885 in Copenhagen, Denmark. He belonged to a highly influential and well educated family. His father, Professor Christian Bohr taught physiology at the University of Copenhagen, while his mother, Ellen Adler, came from a prominent Jew family. It was his father who was greatly responsible for awakening his interest in physics. In his adolescence, he played for Copenhagen-based Akademisk Boldklub as a footballer.

Bohr received his early education at the *Gammelholm Grammar School.* In 1903, he joined the Copenhagen University, where he initially studied philosophy and mathematics. After he won a prize for an essay on physics, he decided to adopt physics and drop philosophy. He received his Master's degree in Physics in 1909. Bohr completed his Doctorate in 1911. Later, he conducted experiments under the guidance of *Professor J. J. Thomson at the Trinity College, Cambridge* as a *post doctorate student.*

Professor Bohr got married in 1912, to Margrethe Nørlund. They had six sons, out of which one died in an accident and the other died in childhood. One of his sons, Aage Bohr, carried Niels' work forward and became a physicist. Aage was also awarded the Nobal *Prize in Physics in 1975.*

Contributions & Achievements:

In 1913, *Bohr's model of atomic structure* was published which became the basis of the famous quantum theory. In 1916, Niels Bohr became a Professor at the University of Copenhagen and later founded the Institute of *Theoretical Physics in 1921.* Bohr's institute became the headquarter for *theoretical physicists* and most of the best known physicists contributed there.

Due to security reasons, Niels Bohr assumed the name of 'Nicholas baker' for the top-secret Manhattan Project in New Mexico, America. Soon after the World War II, Bohr started advocating the peaceful use of nuclear energy in Copenhagen.

'The Bohr model of the atom', 'The shell model of the atom', 'The correspondence principle', 'The liquid drop model of the atomic nucleus', the identification of uranium isotope and 'The principle of complementarity' are some of his major contributions the field of physics and chemistry.

Bohr died on November 18, 1962, at the age of 77 because of a heart failure. He is buried in the Assistens Kierkegaard in Copenhagen, Denmark. In 1965, in the honour of Bohr, the Institute of Physics at the University of Copenhagen changed its name to the *Niels Bohr Institute.* The chemical element, 'Bohrium' and 'Asteroid 3948 Bohr' being named after him are few of his legacies.

Nikola Tesla

1856 – 1943

Nikola Tesla was a Serbian-American engineer and inventor who is highly regarded in the energy history for his development of Alternating Current (AC) electrical systems. He also made extraordinary contributions in the fields of Electromagnetism and Wireless Radio Communications.

Nikola Tesla was born in the Croatian town of Smiljan (Austrian Empire) in 1856 to a priest father. He studied electrical engineering at the Austrian Polytechnic in Graz and later attended the Charles-Ferdinand University in Prague. Unfortunately, his father died early, and he had to leave the university after completing only one term.

Tesla accepted a job under Tivadar Puskás in a Budapest telegraph company in 1880. He was later promoted the post of a to chief electrician and later engineer for the company. He then moved to Paris to work for the *Continental Edison Company* as an engineer.

After moving to New York, United States, Tesla worked for *Thomas Alva Edison,* but the two did not get along well. He started working with *George Westinghouse* in 1885. There, he devised an electrical distribution system that employed the Alternating Current (AC).

Contributions & Achievements:

Tesla made public the first successful wireless energy transfer to power electronic devices in 1891.

Probably Tesla's most important contribution to energy history is the use of Alternating Current (AC). The Westinghouse Electric Company was the first to implement this technology by lighting the World Colombian Exposition in Chicago in 1893. It proved to be a more efficient and effective method as compared to the direct current (DC) system of Edison to transport electricity in a grid. The technology quickly became the basis for most of the modern electricity distribution systems. Besides the AC system, Tesla helped in the development of *generators and turbine design.* The earliest *demonstration fluorescent lighting* was also his accomplishment.

Nikola Tesla continued his research work on *electricity generation* and *turbine design* in his later life. Even at 81, he claimed to have completed a *'dynamic theory of gravity'* – something which was never published. He died in New York City of a heart thrombus in January 1943. He was 86 years old.

Noam Chomsky

Noam Chomsky is an eminent American theoretical linguist, cognitive scientist and philosopher, who radically changed the *arena of linguistics* by assuming language as a uniquely human, biologically based cognitive capacity. He suggested that *innate traits in the human brain give birth to both language and grammar.* The most important figure in "cognitive revolution" and "analytic philosophy", Chomsky's wide-ranging influence also extends to *computer science and mathematics.*

Avram Noam Chomsky was born in Philadelphia, Pennsylvania in 1928. Both his parents were prominent Hebrew scholars. He entered the University of Pennsylvania in 1945, where he achieved a *bachelor's degree in linguistics in 1949*, a *master's degree in 1951*, and *later earned his doctorate in 1955.*

Contributions & Achievements:

Noam Chomsky became a member of the faculty of the Massachusetts Institute of Technology and performed his services at MIT as a visiting professor. Influenced by the ideas of his mentor, Zellig Harris, Chomsky published his famous work, '*Syntactic Structures*', in 1957. During that era, concepts regarding the origin of language were inspired by the behaviourist ideas, for instance, those of renowned Swedish psychologist B. F. Skinner, who advocated that newborn babies had a *blank mind (tabula rasa*) and that children acquired language by means of learning and mimickry.

Chomsky rejected that belief and argued that human beings were in fact born with the innate ability to realise the generative grammars that constitute every human language. Children make use of this innate ability to learn the languages that they are exposed to.

Chomsky established his *linguistic theory in 1965* with 'Aspects of the Theory of Syntax', and in 1975, with 'The Logical Structure of Linguistic Theory'. Later works in cognitive science supported his claims. The influence of Chomsky on linguistics is similar to that of Charles Darwin on evolution and biology. His ideas have significant logical implications for various subjects of psychology, and also extends to cognitive science, anthropology, sociology and neurology.

Noam Chomsky won an *honorary fellowship at the Literary and Historical Society* in 2005. Two years later, he received The Uppsala University Honourary Doctor's degree in 2007, named after Carolus Linnaeus. He was honoured with the *President's Medal* from the Literary *and Debating Society of the National University of Ireland, Galway* in 2008. Chomsky has been serving as an honourary member of The *International Association of Professional Translators and Interpreters* (IAPTI), since 2009.

Omar Khayyam

1048-1131

Omar Khayyam was one of the major mathematicians and astronomers of the medieval period. He was acknowledged as the author of the most important treatise on algebra before modern times. This is reflected in his *Treatise on Demonstration of Problems of Algebra* giving a geometric method for solving cubic equations by intersecting a hyperbola with a circle. His significance as a philosopher and teacher, and his few remaining philosophical works, has not received the same attention as his scientific and poetic writings.

Omar Khayyam was born on May 18, 1048 AD in Iran. Omar Khayyam's full name was *Ghiyath al-Din Abu'l-Fath Umar Ibn Ibrahim Al-Nisaburi al-Khayyami.* He was born into a family of tent makers. He spent part of his childhood in the town of Balkh, northern Afghanistan, studying under Sheik Muhammad Mansuri. Later on, he studied under Imam Mowaffaq Nishapuri, who was considered one of the greatest teachers of the Khorassan region. Khayyam had notable works in geometry, particularly on the theory of proportions.

Contributions & Achievements:

He was a Persian polymath, mathematician, philosopher, astronomer, physician and poet. He wrote treatises on mechanics, geography and music. The treatise of Khayyam can be considered as the first treatment of *parallels axiom* which is not based on petition principle but on more intuitive postulate. Khayyam refutes the previous attempts by other Greek and Persian mathematicians to prove the proposition. and he refused the use of motion in geometry.

Khayyam was the mathematician who noticed the importance of a *general binomial theorem.* The argument supporting the claim that Khayyam had a general binomial theorem is based on his ability to extract roots. Khayyam was part of a panel that introduced several reforms to the Persian calendar. On March 15, 1079, Sultan Malik Shah, accepted this corrected calendar as the official Persian calendar.

Khayyam's poetic work has eclipsed his fame as a mathematician. He has written about a thousand four-line verses or quatrains. In the English-speaking world, he was introduced through the *Rubáiyát of Omar Khayyam* which are rather free-wheeling English translations by Edward FitzGerald (1809-1883). Khayyam's personal beliefs are discernible from his poetic verses. In his own writings, Khayyam rejected strict religious structure and a literalist conception of the afterlife.

Khayyam taught for decades the philosophy of Avicenna, especially in his hometown Nishapur, till his death. Khayyam, the philosopher can be understood from two rather distinct sources. One is through his *Rubaiyat* and the other through his own works in light of the intellectual and social conditions of his time. The latter could be informed by the evaluations of Khayyam's works by scholars and philosophers, such as Bayhaqi, Nezami Aruzi, and Zamakhshari and Sufi poets and writers Attar Nishapuri and Najmeddin Razi. As a mathematician, *Khayyam* has made fundamental contributions to the Philosophy of mathematics especially in the context of *Persian Mathematics* and *Persian Philosophy* with which, most of the other Persian scientists and philosophers, such as Avicenna, Biruni and Tusi are associated.

Omer Khayyam passed away on December the 4th, 1131 in Nishapur, *Persia* now known as *Iran*.

Otto Hahn

Otto Hahn was a German chemist and researcher, who is widely considered to be one of the most influential nuclear chemists in history. He pioneered the fields of *radiochemistry* and *radioactivity*. Also known as *'the father of nuclear chemistry',* Hahn crusaded against the use of nuclear weapons after World War II. As an influential citizen of the Federal Republic of Germany, he had also strongly opposed Jewish persecution by the Nazis.

Hahn was born in Frankfurt, Germany, in 1879 to a rich entrepreneur named Heinrich Hahn. He developed an interest in chemistry at 15, though his father wanted him to study architecture. He studied chemistry and *mineralogy* and later received his *doctorate in organic chemistry* from the University of Marburg in 1901, where hs also worked for two years as an assistant to his doctoral supervisor, Theodor Zincke.

Contributions & Achievements:

Hahn accepted a job at the University *College of London in 1904,* where the famous discovery of *radiothorium*, a new radioactive substance, took place. He continued his pioneering research in *nuclear chemistry* at McGill University in Montreal, where he discovered *radioactinium*, a radioactive isotope of thorium.

He went back to Germany in 1907 and joined the University of Berlin as a lecturer. Hahn made his most significant contribution to energy history in 1938. While working with Fritz Strassmann, a fellow chemist, he discovered that the element, barium was produced when uranium atoms were bombarded with neutrons.

Actually, Hahn and Strassmann had come upon nuclear fission, the primary chemical process involved in a nuclear reaction. This legendary discovery indirectly helped to develop the *atomic bomb* and *nuclear energy*. For his discovery of *nuclear fission*, Hahn was awarded the *Nobel Prize in 1944*. He went forward with his research and the development and separation of new elements using the process of nuclear fission.

Otto Hahn joined the *Kaiser Wilhelm Society (KWG)* in 1946. He was the last president of the institution. Hahn was also the founding president of the Max Planck Society (MPG), where he performed his duties from 1948 to 1960.

Hahn died on July 28, 1968. He was 89 years old.

Paul Dirac

Paul Dirac (full name: Paul Adrien Maurice Dirac) was an English theoretical physicist and mathematician, who is widely regarded to be one of the *founders of quantum mechanics* and *quantum electrodynamics.* Noted for his 1928 *relativistic quantum theory of the electron*, and for predicting of the existence of anti-particles, Dirac shared the *1933 Nobel Prize for Physics* with Erwin Schrödinger.

Born on August 8, 1902 in Bristol, England, Paul Dirac's father was an immigrant from Saint-Maurice, Switzerland who taught French. He attended the Bishop Road Primary School, and later the Merchant Venturers' Technical College, where his father was a French teacher. Dirac acquired a degree in electrical engineering at the University of Bristol in 1921.

Contributions & Achievements:

When the theory of relativity became famous in 1919, he gained an interest in the technical aspect of relativity. Dirac joined the University of Cambridge as a research student in 1923, where he further developed Heisenberg's unpublished hypothesis regarding quantum mechanics.

Paul Dirac is known as one of the greatest physicists in history. His contributions laid the groundwork for quantum mechanics and quantum electrodynamics. He formulated quantum field theory after reworking his own Dirac equation as a many-body equation. The work predicted the existence of antimatter and matter–antimatter annihilation. Dirac was the first physicist to devise quantum electrodynamics. He also discovered the magnetic monopole solutions.

Dirac was made Lucasian professor of mathematics at the University of Cambridge in 1932, where he taught for almost 37 years. He began indepedent research in the *area of quantum theory in 1925.* A few years later, he published his famous work *'The principles of quantum mechanics' (1932)*, for which he shared the *1933 Nobel Prize for physics* with Erwin Schrödinger. He was appointed a *fellow of the Royal Society in 1930.*

Paul Dirac died on October 20, 1984 in Tallahassee, Florida. He was 82 years old.

Paul Ehrlich

1854 – 1915

Paul Ehrlich was a German scientist whose influence extended across diverse fields, including immunology, haematology and chemotherapy. Ehrlich discovered the first *practical treatment for syphilis*, for which he shared the *1908 Nobel Prize for Physiology or Medicine* with *Russian biologist Élie Metchnikoff.*

Born in 1854 into an affluent Jewish family, Paul Ehrlich developed an interest in the process of staining cells with chemical dyes as a youth. He studied medicine at the Universities of Strasbourg, Breslau, Freiburg and Leipzig. Ehrlich earned his medical degree from the University of Leipzig in 1878.

During his experimentation with *cellular staining,* Ehrlich noticed that chemical reactions took place in cells and that these reactions were the cause of cellular processes. He concluded that chemical agents could cure diseased cells and fight infectious agents, an idea that radically changed therapeutics and medical diagnostics. Ehrlich coined the term 'chemotherapy'. He also detected a particular chemical reaction in the urine of typhoid patients and made important contributions for the treatment of various eye diseases.

Contributions & Achievements:

Ehrlich was appointed a head physician at Charité Hospital, Berlin, where he came up with an exclusive staining method to recognise the *tuberculosis bacillus.* Ehrlich also differentiated the various kinds of blood cells of the body, and by doing so, became one of the founders of haematology. Ehrlich discovered the application of *methylene blue* for curing *nervous disorders.*

He published about *37 scientific papers* between 1879 and 1885. Perhaps, his most influential work, 'Das Sauerstoff-Bedürfniss des

Organismus' (The Requirement of the Organism for Oxygen), published in 1885, maintained that oxygen consumption changes with various types of tissues and that these changes form a measure of the intensity of vital cell processes.

Paul Ehrlich shared the *Nobel Prize for Physiology or Medicine* with *Russian biologist Élie Metchnikoff* in 1908. He died of a stroke in Hesse, Germany, on August 20, 1915. Ehrlich was 61 years old.

Pierre Curie

1859 – 1906

Pierre Curie was a French physical chemist who discovered *radium and polonium,* while studying *radioactivity* with his wife, Marie Curie. Widely considered to be one of the founders of modern physics, he pioneered the fields of *crystallography, magnetism and piezoelectricity.* Curie shared the *1903 the Nobel Prize in Physics with his wife for their* work on radiation.

Born in Paris, France on May 15, 1859, *Pierre Curie was a childhood prodigy.* He showed an extraordinary aptitude for mathematics and geometry. Curie completed the equivalent of a higher degree when he was only 18, but failed to pursue a doctorate due to some financial problems. He instead accepted a job as a *laboratory instructor.*

Contributions & Achievements:

Pierre Curie is widely credited to be one of the founders of modern physics. As a young researcher, his work had already brought important discoveries related to *heat waves, crystals, magnetism and symmetry.* He formulated the Curie's law before he married Marie Sklowdowska in 1895. The Curies, the husband and wife, together discovered polonium and radium, while conducting research in radioactivity.

Together with Henri Becquerel, the Curies shared the *1903 Nobel Prize in Physics* for their revolutionary work on radioactivity.

Pierre Curie died in a street accident in Paris on April 19, 1906. He was only 46 years old.

Pierre-Simon Laplace

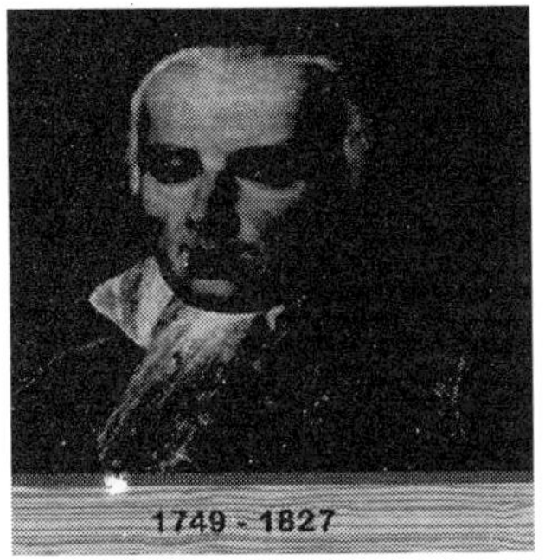

Pierre-Simon Laplace was a prominent French mathematical physicist and astronomer of the 19th century, who made crucial contributions in the arena of planetary motion by applying Sir Isaac Newton's theory of gravitation to the entire Solar System. His work regarding the theory of probability and statistics is considered pioneering, and has influenced a whole new generation of mathematicians.

Pierre-Simon Laplace entered the Caen University when he was only 16 and he soon developed a strong interest in mathematics. When he was only 19, he moved to Paris, without finishing his degree, to work as a professor of mathematics at the École Militaire with the fellow mathematician Jean-le-Rond D'Alembert. Five years later, Laplace had already written 13 scientific papers regarding integral calculus, mechanics and physical astronomy, which gained him fame and acclaim all over France.

Contributions & Achievements:

Pierre-Simon Laplace is highly regarded for his influential five-volume treatise, 'Traité de mécanique céleste' (Celestial mechanics; 1799-1825), which developed a strong mathematical understanding of the motion of the heavenly bodies, including several anomalies and inequalities that were noticed in their orbits. Laplace suggested that the nature of the universe is completely deterministic.

Laplace heavily contributed in the development of *differential equations, difference equations, probability and statistics*. His 1812 work, 'Théorie analytique des probabilités' (Analytic theory of probability) furthered the subjects of probability and statistics significantly.

Laplace was made a member of the *Paris Academic des Sciences* in

1773, where he assumed a senior position in 1785. He was given the duty of standardising all European weights and measures.

His work on *celestial mechanics* is considered revolutionary. He established that the small perturbations observed in the orbital motion of the planets will always remain small, constant and self-correcting. He was the earliest astronomer to suggest the idea that the solar system originated from the contraction and cooling of a large rotating, and consequently flattened, nebula of incandescent gas. *Laplace published his famous work on probability in 1812.* He supplied his own definition of probability and applied it to justify the *fundamental mathematical manipulations.*

Laplace died in Paris, France, on March 5, 1827. He was 77 years old. It is impossible to overstate the influence Laplace had on the progress of the *Mathematical Theory of Mechanics.* Various fundamental concepts, for instance, the *Laplace Operator* in potential theory and the *Laplace Transform* in the study of *Differential Equations*, are named after him.

Prafulla Chandra Ray

1861 - 1944

Prafulla Chandra Ray, one of the first *Indian chemical researchers,* studied at the prestigious Edinburgh University. After graduating from university, he took a position as a Chemistry Professor at the *Presidency College in 1889.*

Berthelot who was a very famous chemist, helped and encouraged him with his *admirable research in Ayurveda.*

Contributions & Achievements:

In 1902, his research work of *History of Hindu Chemistry* was published. In 1892, he established the *Bengal Chemical and Pharmaceutical* Works that incredibly flourished under Ray's management.

Ray represented many Indian universities at international seminars and congresses. He got elected as the Indian Science Congress President in 1920.

Prafulla Chandra Ray wanted to use the marvels of science for lifting up the masses.

Many of his articles on science got published in renowned journals of his time. *Ray was a very passionate and devoted social worker and he participated eagerly and actively in helping out the famine struck people of Bengal in 1922.*

He promoted the *khadi material* and also set up many *cottage industries.*

He was a true rationalist and was completely against the caste system or other irrational social systems, etc. He persistently carried on this work of social reformation till he passed away.

Pythagoras

570-495 BC

Pythagoras, a very famous *philosopher* from Greece and also a *religious teacher,* was born in c. 575 B.C on the Samos Island. He was the leader of the school of thought that believed that *souls could be transmigrated and also developed it as a universal principle.*

His father was Mnesarchus. He ran to the South of Italy to get away from the oppression of the Polycrates who had come to power in 538 B.C. It is said that he has also been to Babylon and Egypt. He and his supporters came into power in the south of Italy in Croton. That's where Pythagoras established a school for new sect. It is predicted that Pythagoreans participated in the home government so that they could preach people to lead pure and simple lives as per their teachings. But, unfortunately the enemies attacked the Pythagoreans and the whole sect was eradicated. So the Pythagoreans were either evicted from Italy or they left the town willingly after they were attacked. He passed away in c. 495 B.C. in Metapontum.

Contributions & Achievements:

Religious Teachings

Pythagoras and his supporters contributed a lot to both *science and religion.* The teachings he gave about religion were based on the *principle of metempsychosis* according to which the belief was that the soul was eternal and that it was intended to be reborn until it could set itself free from the phase of wholesomeness of its life.

Pythagoreanism was different from other systems of philosophy. It did not just seek the truth of life but also gave preaching about leading the way of life till final destination. This aspect made it more similar to mysterious religions than that to philosophy. Many beliefs taught were unthinkable or supernatural that came up from various sources like sympathetic magic, folk rituals and Greek traditional beliefs that were held by them, *while they developed extremely rational and imaginative systems of science.*

Another important aspect of this theory was relationship of the entire life. It was believed that the spirit was present in animals as well as vegetables but there is no proof about this that it was believed by Pythagoras that he believed that spirits could be born in the form of vegetables or plants. He said that he had heard his friend's voice in the form of a dog's howl. It was said that the number of lives as each soul would be born was infinite. This all came from their religious teachings. Pythagoras himself said to have remembered four diverse lives. The followers of Pythagoras and the sect joined into this confidentiality but it was later said that the commands were not observed devotedly.

Mathematical Teachings

The parts between the Unlimited and the Limited were set by the Pythagoreans. It is assumed that Pythagoras himself devised the universal principle, and was a number that gave limited shape to matter. It was his research on the musical intervals that led to discover that the main intervals, that fell amid the initial four integers, could also be expressed in the form of numerical ratio. He also came up with a theory that the summation of the initial four integers is 10 and gripped the complete nature of the number.

Pythagoreans' work regarding the 'Tetractys of the Decad' was so respected that people preferred to oath by this rather than their gods. The famous theorem of the right angled triangles that was discovered by Pythagoras has already been found in the scripts from the time of Hammurabi, a king of Babylon. Still, Pythagoras did some remarkable work in arranging and organising the knowledge of mathematics.

Pythagoras concluded the two contradictions, unlimited and limited, as vital principles. The evenness or oddness of Numericals is equated with the Unlimited and the Limited, just as plurality and one, female and male, left and right, movement and motionlessness, crooked and straight, darkness and light, oblong and square, and bad and good. It was not clear whether there were one or more reasons for setting out these categories.

Cosmological Views

The Pythagoreans came up with cosmology and had different views from their attendants. It was only because of their knowledge of Mathematics and beliefs of religion. Their most important aspect was that the planet, Earth was the shape of the sphere and it rotated in the centre place in the universe. They believed that there was fire in the centre of the system but it was not visible to the people as they said their side of earth was turned away from it. They also believed that the sun was reflected from this fire and the rest five planets were far away. They had to take longer routes around. It is unknown that how much part of this theory was given out by Pythagoras on his own. Later it was said by many people that this theory was given out by Philolaos although it was the whole group of people who circulated this view.

Pythagoras was very well known for his teachings of religion and mathematics in the western world. He made a very good religious teacher and many of the ancient believes in Greece are based on teachings of Pythagoras.

Rachel Carson

"Through all these new, imaginative and creative approaches to the problem of sharing our earth with other creatures, there runs a constant theme, the awareness that we are dealing with life with living populations and all their pressures and counter-pressures, their surges and recessions. Only by taking account of such life forces and by cautiously seeking to guide them into channels favourable to ourselves can we hope to achieve a reasonable accommodation between the insect hordes and ourselves." – Rachel Louise Carson

American marine biologist, writer and naturalist, Rachel Louise Carson is famous for advancing the global environmental movement through her writings. She is regarded as one of the most influential people of the 20th century.

Born on May 27, 1907 on a small family farm near Springdale, Pennsylvania, Rachel Carson was the youngest of the three children. As a child, she spent a lot of time exploring the forests and streams around her farm, developing a great passion for nature. She became a devoted writer and published her first story at the age of eleven in the St. *Nicholas Magazine.*

Carson received her early education at a small school of Springdale and then completed high school in nearby Parnassus, Pennsylvania, graduating in 1925 at the top of her class of 44 students. The same year, she entered the Pennsylvania College for Women (later the Chatham College) as English major determined to become a writer. However inspired by an outstanding biology teacher at her college, she switched her major to biology.

Contributions & Achievements:

After graduation, she held a summer study fellowship at the *Marine*

Biological Laboratory at Woods Hole, Massachusetts. There she fell in love with the ocean, which later became the topic of several of her best-selling books. She then entered *Johns Hopkins University* (on the basis of scholarship and received upon her graduation from Pennsylvania College) and completed her masters in marine zoology, while serving as a teaching subordinate and part-time instructor in biology at Johns Hopkins and the University of Maryland.

Carson's distinction in both writing and biology earned her a part-time position with the *U.S. Bureau of Fisheries* in 1935, in a temporary job, where she wrote radio scripts on marine life. Her articles were published regularly by the *Baltimore Sun* and other of its syndicated papers. From 1936 to 1952, she became a full-time employee of the *Fish and Wildlife Service (FWS),* moving into positions that further polished her skills as a *writer and editor*. She was finally appointed editor-in-chief of the information division.

Carson published her first and favourite book in 1941, *'Under the Sea-Wind': A Naturalist's Picture of Ocean Life'*. Her second book, '*The Sea Around Us*', was published in 1951 and explored the origins and geological aspects of the sea, and this was also published. It won the *National Book Award,* selling more than 200,000 copies. In 1955, upon completion of *The Edge of the Sea,* Carson began focussing on her growing concern over the effects of chemicals and pesticides on the environment. Her last and perhaps the most famous book, '*Silent Spring*' was published in 1956. It awakened the society to a responsibility to other forms of life.

This great woman died from cancer on April 14, 1964. Her interment is situated at the *Parklawn Memorial Park* and *Menorah Gardens* in *Rockville, Maryland.*

René Descartes

1596 – 1650

René Descartes was a highly influential French philosopher, scientist and mathematician, who is widely considered to be one of the celebrated geniuses of the 17th century. His legendary experiment of presenting a geometrical point using a pair of ordered numbers (now called *coordinate geometry)* almost kick-started modern mathematics.

The famous skepticism of Descartes, that distrusted every belief but his own conscious thinking, is usually credited as the terminus a quo for modern philosophy. He is also known as the 'Father of Modern Philosophy'.

Born in Indre-et-Loire, France in 1596 to a parliamentarian, Descartes graduated from the Jesuit Collège Royal Henry-Le-Grand. He later acquired a degree in law from the University of Poitiers in 1616.

He was recruited in the army of Maurice of Nassau in the Dutch Republic, where he managed to make some time to study mathematics, physics and philosophy, nonetheless.

Contributions & Achievements:

Descartes was one of the most influential persons in the *Scientific Revolution. He virtually* condensed the range and variety in the World by his well-known phrase; 'matter in motion.' He wrote various books and papers about optics, and examined the rainbows. He declared there was no vacuum, but supported *momentum conservation.* Descartes also devised the *principle of inertia.* A supporter of the *wave theory of light* and *vortex theory for planets,* he thought of the universe and the human body as a giant machine. He is also described as the 'father of analytical geometry'.

His most significant philosophical position was connected with the *mind-body dichotomy.* Descartes explained that mind was external to the physical body into which it entered through the pineal gland. He thought that science is an activity of the observing mind (res cogitans) to perceive an observed objective reality (ref extensa). Using one concise phrase, 'cogito ergo sum' (I think, therefore I am), he changed the whole direction of Western philosophy. Descartes is credited as the first thinker to offer a philosophical framework for the natural sciences. His theological beliefs became controversial at the time and faced direct opposition from the Pope.

The theories and treatises of Descartes immensely influenced countless aspects of the physical and scientific world.

René Descartes died of pneumonia on February 11, 1650 in Stockholm, Sweden, where he was invited there to teach the *Queen Christina.*

Richard Feynman

Richard Phillips Feynman was a prominent American scientist, widely considered to be one of the greatest and most influential theoretical physicists in history. Feynman revolutionised the field of *quantum mechanics* and formulated the *theory of quantum electrodynamics*. He won the *Nobel Prize for Physics in 1965.*

Born in 1918 in Brooklyn, Richard Feynman's parents were of Jewish descent. Feyrman earned his Ph.D. from the Princeton University in 1942.

Contributions & Achievements:

Richard Feynman was one of the key figures in the Manhattan Project at Los Alamos during World War II. After the war, Feynman accepted teaching positions at Cornell and the *California Institute of Technology.* He was awarded the *1965 Nobel Prize in Physics* for successfully resolving problems related to the theory of *quantum electrodynamics.*

Feynman also formulated a mathematical theory that dealt with the phenomenon of superfluidity in liquid helium. In collaboration with Murray Gell-Mann, he extensively studied weak interactions, such as *beta decay.* Feynman played a vital role in the development of the quark theory by presenting his *parton model* of *high energy proton collision processes.*

Feynman is credited with the introduction of fundamental computational techniques and notations into physics. The Feynman diagrams have radically changed the way in which the basic physical processes are conceptualised and calculated. As a legendary educator, Feynman was awarded the *Oersted Medal for Teaching in 1972.*

On a mission to increase the understanding of physics among the general public, Feynman wrote, "The Character of Physical Law" and "Q.E.D: The Strange Theory of Light and Matter". He also published various advanced works that have become definitive references and textbooks for scholars and students alike.

Richard Feynman died of abdominal cancer on February 15, 1988, in Los Angeles. He was 69 years old.

Rita Levi-Montalcini

1909 - PRESENT

"Above all, don't fear difficult moments. The best comes from them." – Rita Levi Montalcini

Today women have occupied a greater name in the field of science, proving that they are capable of equating men in their abilities to conduct scientific research. They have taken significant positions in the scientific field as compared to the more traditional roles: mother, wife, and homemaker that existed in the past centuries.

Contributions & Achievements:

Italian Neurophysiologist, Rita Levi-Montalcini is one exceptional woman, who through her pioneering contribution and hard work has set an amazing example for other women to follow her footsteps. She won the *1986 Nobel Prize for physiology or medicine* which she shared with the *biochemist, Stanley Cohen*, for their discovery of *nerve growth factor (NGF),* a protein that causes developing cells to grow by stimulating the *surrounding nerve tissue.* At 101 years, she has the stamina that many younger people might envy. On her workdays, Rita gives equal time to her namesake brain research laboratory and her foundation to support African women with potential for scientific accomplishment.

Rita Levi-Montalcini was born on April 22, 1909 in Turin to a Sephardic Jewish family. She was the youngest child of her parents, Adamo Levi, an electrical engineer and talented mathematician, and Adele Montalcini, a painter. She enrolled in the University of Turin in 1930 to study medicine, despite her father's belief that women should not pursue careers. After completing her graduation in 1936, she went to work as Giuseppe Levi's assistant, but her academic career was cut short by *Benito Mussolini's 1938 Manifesto of Race* and following the introduction of laws barring Jews from intellectual and professional careers.

"This led me to the joy of working, no longer, unfortunately, in university institutes, but in a bedroom."

Dr. Levi-Montalcini simply constructed a laboratory in her own home and conducted research in secrecy. For the next few years, she conducted experiments on chicken embryos, she would cook and eat the remaining yolks. While acting as a doctor in Italian refugee camps, she took out time to publish her research on the sources of nerve constructs.

Subsequent to the Germans invasion of Italy, she left for Florence and lived underground with her family. When the war ended, she accepted a one-year residency at Washington University in St Louis, but stayed more than three decades. She worked together with zoologist Viktor Hamburger and after sometime with biochemist Stanley Cohen, pioneering the Nerve-Growth Factor (NGF) and Epidermal Growth Factor (EGF). Levi-Montalcini and Cohen won the ***Nobel Prize*** **for** ***Medicine*** **in 1986.**

Indeed, the latter part of *Levi-Montalcini's life consists of a long list of scientific prizes and honours.* In addition to her continuing research, she is an FAO Goodwill Ambassador (1999) and an Italian Senator For life (2001).

"It is imperative that we support FAO's campaign, urging young people, who more than adults enjoy the ability to spring into action, to play what could be a decisive role in the elimination of this tragic reality. I ask you to join us by participating in FAO's campaign against world hunger".

Robert Bosch

Robert August Bosch was a German inventor, engineer and industrialist who founded the Robert Bosch GmbH, one of the world's leading engineering firms, in 1886. Robert Bosch is also noted for inventing the *spark plug* and the *electrical magneto for automobiles.*

Born on September 23, 1861, near Ulm in Württemberg, south-western Germany, Robert Bosch attended the Technical University at Stuttgart. He also received training in mechanics in Ulm, Great Britain and the United States.

Contributions & Achievements:

Robert Bosch established the *Robert Bosch GmbH Corporation,* one of the leading producers of automotive technology who also manufactured numerous other products.

Bosch made salient contributions to the expansion of the automobile industry and related sectors.

Bosch started his own company, "Workshop for Precision Mechanics and Electrical Engineering", when he was only 25. He invented a magneto for gas engines in 1887, which was used in an automobile engine almost ten years later.

He also invented the first spark plug, an invention which revolutionised the operation of automobiles. His company largely benefitted from the war, but Bosch open-heartedly donated more than ten million marks back to the German public.

Bosch Industries faced severe crisis after the war due to the depressing economic downfall, but the company massively restructured in 1927, expanding into the manufacture of cameras, power tools, television sets, refrigerators and radios.

Robert Bosch died on March 12, 1942 in Stuttgart, Germany, of complications resulting from an inflammation of the middle ear. He was 80 years old.

Robert Boyle

1627 – 1691

Robert Boyle was an Anglo-Irish natural philosopher, scientist and theological writer. As one of the early pioneers of modern experimental scientific method, *Boyle's contributions ranged over a number of subjects, including chemistry, physics, medicine, hydrostatics, natural history and the earth sciences.*

Born in Ireland on 25 January, 1627 to a wealthy and influential family, Robert Boyle's father, *Richard Boyle, was Lord Treasurer of the Kingdom of Ireland.* Boyle received the best education from various prestigious schools, including Eton, where he studied philosophy, religion, mathematics and the latest trends in physics and chemistry.

After studying a few years under the local parson, Boyle gained a strong interest in science. He gathered many prominent scientists from various fields of science, who had weekly meetings in Oxford and London. The group later became the *Royal Society of London.* Boyle was elected its president, but he declined the position as the required oath breached his strict religious beliefs.

Contributions & Achievements:

Boyle was the earliest-known scientist to really publish his works. He carefully collected his experiments, along with his failures and findings. His 1660 scientific paper, '*The Spring and Weight of Air*', mentioned the usage of an improved vacuum pump of a custom design. Boyle significantly modified the clumsy and inefficient pump of Von Guericke, which needed two men to operate, and with great effort. In Boyle's new design, vacuum could be sustained with only one operator in a very efficient manner.

Boyle carried out various experiments which helped him in the discovery of the relationship between pressure and volume of gases. This resulted in the 'Boyle-Mariotte Law' which implies that if the temperature is constant, the volume of a gas is inversely proportional to the pressure. The phrase, 'chemical analysis' was also coined by him.

In that era, it was widely believed that elements like salt and water could be broken down no further. Boyle largely opposed the *theories of basic elements.*

Boyle was a very pious person and died, having never married, from paralysis in London on December 30, 1691. He was 64 years old.

Robert Bunsen

1811 – 1899

Robert Bunsen (In full: Robert Wilhelm Eberhard Bunsen) was an *eminent German chemist.* Bunsen, along with his fellow scientist, Gustav Kirchhoff, is credited with the breakthrough discovery (1859) that *each element emits a light of characteristic wavelength.* The event caused a revolution in the field of *spectrum analysis,* and later led to the *discovery of two alkali-group metals,* namely *cesium and rubidium.* He is also noted for developing the famous Bunsen Burner, with the help of his assistant, Peter Desaga.

Born at Göttingen, Germany in 1811, Robert Bunsen's father taught modern philology at the University of Göttingen. He earned a Ph.D. in chemistry at the same university in 1830, and himself became a successful professor at the Universities of Marburg, Breslau and Heidelberg.

Contributions & Achievements:

Robert Bunsen's research on the highly toxic arsenic-containing *compound cacodyl in 1837 was one of his first acclaimed works.* He extensively studied *emission spectra of heated elements,* with Gustav Kirchhoff, which helped them discover *caesium in 1860,* and *rubidium in 1861.* As one of the early pioneers of *photochemistry and organoarsenic chemistry,* Bunsen formulated various *gas-analytical methods.* He built the Bunsen burner with his laboratory assistant, Peter Desaga, in 1855; an invention which greatly bettered the form of laboratory burners.

Bunsen is also credited with the 1841 invention of the carbon-zinc electric cell, as well as *the grease-spot photometer* in 1844, which measured the light produced by the cell. He obtained magnesium in the metallic state for the first time and analysed its physical and chemical properties. A few other inventions by Bunsen include the *filter pump* in 1868, the *ice calorimeter* in 1870, and the *vapour calorimeter* in 1887.

Robert Bunsen died in Heidelberg, south-west Germany on August 16, 1899. He was 88 years old.

Robert Goddard

1882 – 1945

Robert Goddard (In full: Robert Hutchings Goddard) was an eminent American physicist and inventor. Widely regarded as the founder of *modern rocketry,* Goddard created the first *liquid-fueled rocket.* He published 'A Method of Reaching Extreme Altitudes' in 1919, a classic treatise that remains the most influential work in the 20th century rocket science.

Born in Worcester, Massachusetts in 1882, Robert Goddard earned a B.S. degree in Physics from Worcester Polytechnic Institute in 1908, and an A.M. degree in Physics from the Clark University in 1910. After receiving his Ph.D. in 1911, he became a very popular physics professor.

Contributions & Achievements:

Robert Goddard was the first scientist to transcend the traditional focus from the substance to be ignited to oxygen, *the element essential for combustion.* He established that rockets based on atmospheric oxygen can never fly in space, where the lack of oxygen will eliminate combustion. Goddard also discovered that the rate of combustion depends on the amount of oxygen.

Wernher von Braun, a German physicist and a friend of Goddard, instituted the *German Rocket Society in 1927,* following Goddard's March 1926 launch of a rocket fuelled by *gasoline and liquid oxygen.* The German army started research to create a *long-range missile using liquid propellants* in 1931. Goddard unknowingly assisted the program by answering telephone queries from German engineers. However, by 1939, Nazi aggression alerted him.

From May to July of 1940, Goddard explained the U.S. Army and Navy officials about the German threat and the necessity for the United States to produce its own long-range missiles. Although war planners largely ignored him, thinking that Germany was not capable of launching a missile across the Atlantic, Goddard worked for the navy between 1942 and 1945, as director of research in the Bureau of Aeronautics, creating experimental engines.

Robert Goddard became a consultant for *Curtiss-Wright Corporation,* a leading aircraft firm, in 1943, and director of the *American Rocket Society* in 1944. He died of throat cancer in Baltimore, Maryland, on August 10, 1945. Goddard was 62 years old.

Robert Hooke

1635 – 1703

The British natural philosopher, architect and polymath, *Robert Hooke is perhaps the most neglected natural philosophers of all time despite the significant role he played in the scientific revolution.* His prominent contributions include: The *iris diaphragm in cameras, the universal joint used in motor vehicles, the balance wheel in a watch, the origination of the word* **'cell'** *in biology, etc.* He was the Surveyor of the City of London after the Great Fire of 1666, architect, experimenter, worked in astronomy – yet is acknowledged mostly for the *Hooke's Law.*

His name is somewhat obscure today, due in part to the hostility of his well-known and dominant colleague, Sir Isaac Newton.

Robert was born on the 18th of July 1635 at Freshwater, in the Isle of Wight, England. He was the last of the four children of John Hooke and Mirena Blazer. His father was the minister of the Church of England. Most of his early life, Robert had a poor health due to which he received most of his early education at home from his father, who was also in charge of a local school. As a youth, Robert had a natural curiosity in his surroundings and interest in mechanical works and drawing that he pursued in various ways all through his life.

At the age of thirteen young Hooke was able to enter Westminster School, and from there went to Oxford, where some of the finest scientists in England were working at the time. There he built a good impression with his skills at designing experiments and building equipment. He was appointed as a chemical assistant to Dr Thomas Willis and later met the natural philosopher Robert Boyle, and gained a position as his assistant from about 1655 to 1662.

Contributions & Achievements:

During November 1661, he was appointed the *curator of experiments to the Royal Society* after a proposition made by *Sir Robert Murray. In* 1664, Sir John Cutler settled an annual gratuity of 50 pounds on the Society for mechanical lectureship and in the following year, Robert was nominated professor of geometry in Gresham College, where he later resided. After the *Great Fire of 1666,* he constructed a model for the rebuilding of the city, which was highly approved, although the design of Sir Christopher Wren was preferred.

Hooke's contribution to biology is mainly his book, Micrographia which was published in 1665. He developed the *compound microscope* and the illumination system (one of the best such microscopes of his time) and used it in his demonstrations at the Royal Society's meetings. Using it he also observed organisms as varied as insects, sponges, bryozoans, foraminifera and bird feathers. This was a best-seller during his time.

His other contributions include: the law of elasticity, attracting principles of gravity, and he resolved the problem of the measurement of the distance to a star. It was he who actually created the air pump on which Boyle's experiments could be conducted, etc.

This inspirational founder of modern science passed away on March 3, 1703 in London, England.

Robert Koch

1843 - 1910

Robert Koch was a German physician who is widely credited as one of the founders of *bacteriology* and *microbiology*. He investigated the *anthrax disease cycle in 1876*, and studied the *bacteria that causes tuberculosis in 1882, and cholera in 1883.* He also formulated Koch's postulates. Koch won the *1905 Nobel Prize in Physiology or Medicine.*

Born in 1843 in Glausthal, Germany, Robert Koch was a childhood prodigy. He taught himself to read newspapers when he was only 5. He loved to read *classical literature* and was a *chess expert.* He gained an *interest in science,* while in high school, and decided to study biology. Koch acquired his medical degree from the University of Göttingen, Germany in 1866.

Contributions & Achievements:

Koch developed a strong interest in *pathology and infectious diseases* as a medical student. After working as a physician in many small towns throughout Germany, he volunteered as a *military surgeon* during the *Franco-Prussian war (1870-72).* He was appointed a district medical officer for Wollstein after the war.

His main duty as a medical officer was investigating the spread of infectious bacterial diseases. *Koch was very much interested in the transmission of anthrax from cattle to humans.* Not very happy with the prevailing process of confirming the cause of infectious disease, Koch formulated four criteria in 1890 that must be achieved for establishing a cause of an infectious disease. These rules were termed as 'Koch's postulates' or 'Henle-Koch postulates'. German pathologist Friedrich Gustav Jakob Henle was a collaborator in Koch's research.

Robert Koch's brilliant contributions were acknowledged in 1905, and he won the *Nobel Prize for Physiology or Medicine.* The medical applications of biotechnology still heavily depend on the Koch's principles of affirming the causes of infectious diseases. Koch died in 1910 in the *Black Forest region of Germany.* He was 66 years old.

Rosalind Franklin

1920 – 1958

There is probably no other woman scientist with as much controversy surrounding her life and work as Rosalind Franklin. As a scientist, Miss Franklin was distinguished by extreme clarity and perfection in everything she undertook.

Rosalind Franklin was born in London, England on July 25, 1920. Franklin did extremely well at science and then studied physics and chemistry. When she was 15, she decided to become a scientist.

Rosalind attended St Paul's Girls' School, London, where she displayed great talent in physics and chemistry. From there, she went up to Newnham College, Cambridge in 1938. After graduation in 1941, she was awarded a research scholarship to work on *gas chromatography,* but left in 1942 to work at the British Coal Utilization Research Association, where she worked on the microstructure of coke. As a result of her research, she gained her Doctor of Philosophy (PhD) degree from Cambridge in 1945.

Contributions & Achievements:

Rosalind was asked to join a research group by John Randall. She had been asked to set up a laboratory to study *DNA fibres* using *X-ray crystallography*, where atoms can be precisely mapped by looking at the image of the crystal under an X-ray beam. She had the entire responsibility for determining the structure of DNA. Franklin was able to apply her knowledge of physical chemistry and as a result, she made thinner fibres in order to produce more exact and easier to interpret *X-ray patterns.*

She discovered *A and B forms of DNA,* but concentrated on A as it showed more X-ray spots. This form does not show the *helical structure as well as form* B, which she originally thought of as a ladder with bonds between the bases of the rungs. She did record in her laboratory notebook on the 24th of February, 1953 that she had revised her thinking to that of a *three dimensional helix.*

Twenty-five years after the fact, the first clear recitation of Franklin's contributions appeared. The Double Helix, although it was buried under allegations that Franklin did not know how to interpret her own data but her own publication in the same issue of Nature was the first publication of this more clarified X-ray image of DNA. The *Double Helix* inspired several people to investigate the DNA history and Franklin's contributions but the path to the Double Helix supplied information about original source materials for those that followed. After finishing her portion of the DNA work, Franklin led a pioneering work on the tobacco mosaic and polio viruses.

Rosalind Franklin's critical contributions to the *Crick and Watson model* was – Franklin's lecture at the seminar in 1951, where she presented the two forms of the molecule, type A and type B, and her position, whereby the phosphate units are located in the external part of the molecule. She specified the amount of water to be found in the molecule in accordance with other parts of it, data that has considerable importance in terms of the stability of the molecule. Franklin was the first to discover and formulate these facts, which in fact, constituted the basis for all later attempts to build a model of the molecule.

The rules of the Nobel Prize forbid posthumous nominations and because Rosalind Franklin had died in 1958, she was not eligible for nomination to the Nobel Prize subsequently awarded to Crick, Watson, and Wilkins. The award was for their body of work on nucleic acids and not exclusively for the discovery of the structure of DNA. By the time of the award, Wilkins had been working on the structure of DNA for over ten years, and had done much to confirm the *Watson – Crick Model.* Crick had been working on the *genetic code at Cambridge* and *Watson* had worked on *RNA for some years.*

A debate about the amount of credit due to Franklin continues. What is clear is that she did have a meaningful role in *learning the structure of DNA and that she was a scientist of the first rank.* Franklin also did important research into the micro-structure and properties of coals and other carbons, and spent the last five years of her career elucidating the structure of plant viruses, notably *tobacco mosaic virus.* She died at the age of 37 from complications arising from ovarian cancer.

Rudolf Virchow

Rudolf Virchow was an eminent German pathologist and politician, who is widely regarded as one of the *greatest and most influential physicians in history.* One of the founding fathers of 'social medicine', Virchow developed the concept of *pathological processes,* and by drawing influence from the *cell theory,* analysed the effects of disease in various organs and tissues of the human body.

Rudolf Virchow was born in 1821 to a modest farming family. Virchow proved to be a very bright student, and received a free scholarship for medical training in Berlin. He began his medical studies in 1839, earning his M.D. degree in 1843.

Contributions & Achievements:

The world owes the understanding of the *cellular basis for many diseases,* such as cancer, to Rudolf Virchow. Particularly, passionate about pathological histology, the science of diseased cells and tissues, he published a scientific paper in 1845, that discussed the *oldest known pathological descriptions of leukemia. Virchow was also an fervid social reformer.*

When he was selected to look into a terrible outbreak of typhus fever in Germany, his report highlighted social conditions and blamed the government for the state of affairs that caused the outbreak. He concluded that improper system of sewers, deficiency of clean drinking water and unhygienic conditions led to the spread of the disease. As a consequence, Virchow was suspended for two weeks and he also faced degradation. Virchow, however, stood still in his reform efforts, and carried out on with his scientific research.

An entire pathological institute was established for Virchow at the University of Berlin, where he worked for the rest of his career. He discovered that outside stimuli affected cells, and that diseased cells arise from already diseased and cancerous cells. He focussed on *clinical observations,* physiological experiments and pathological anatomy, occasionally using laboratory animals, operating at the microscopic level. Virchow published probably his most influential work, 'Cellular Pathology', reporting that the cell was the most fundamental unit of disease pathologies, including that of cancer.

Rudolf Virchow was appointed a *foreign member of the Royal Swedish Academy of Sciences in 1861.* He was honoured with the *Copley Medal in 1892.*

Virchow died of heart failure in Berlin on September 5, 1902. He was 80 years old.

Salim Ali

1896 - 1987

Salim Ali, one of the *greatest ornithologists and naturalists of all time,* is also known as the '*birdman of India*'. He was one of the very first scientists to carry out the *systematic bird surveys* in India and abroad. His research work is considered highly influential in the development of ornithology.

As a 10-year-old, Salim once noticed a flying bird and shot it down. Tender at heart, he instantly ran and picked it up. It appeared like a house sparrow, but had a strange yellowish shade on the throat. Curious, he showed the sparrow to his uncle, Amiruddin and questioned him about the bird's kind. Unable to answer, his uncle took him to W.S. Millard, the Honorary Secretary of the Bombay Natural History Society. Amazed at the unusual interest of the young boy, Millard took him to see many stuffed birds. When Salim finally saw a bird similar to the child's bird, he got very excited. After that, the young Salim started visiting the place frequently.

Salim Moizuddin Abdul Ali was born on November 12, 1896. He attended college, but did not receive any university degree. To assist his brother in wolfram mining, he went to Burma, but spent most of his time looking for birds. Soon, he returned back to Bombay.

As soon as Salim returned, he studied zoology, and secured a position of a guide at the museum of the *Bombay Natural History Society.* Only 20 years old, he conducted the visitors and instructed them about the preserved birds. His interest in the living conditions of birds grew even more. Therefore, Salim visited Germany and saw Dr. Irvin Strassman.

He came back to India after one year but his post in the museum had been removed for financial reasons.

Salim Ali, as a married man, required money to make a living, so he joined the museum as a clerk. The job allowed him to carry on with his research. His wife's house at Kihim, a small village near Mumbai, was a tranquil place surrounded by trees, where Salim would spend most of his time researching about the activities of the weaver bird.

Contributions & Achievements:

He published a research paper discussing the nature and activities of the weaver bird in 1930. The piece made him famous and established his name in the field of ornithology. Salim also travelled from place to place to find out more about different species of the birds.

From what he had collected, he published *'The Book of Indian Birds in 1941'* in which he discussed the kinds and habits of Indian birds. The book sold very well for a number of years. *He also collaborated with S. Dillon Ripley, a world-famous ornithologist, in 1948.* The collaboration resulted in the 'Handbook of the Birds of India and Pakistan' (10 Volume Set); a comprehensive book that describes the birds of the subcontinent, their appearance, habitat, breeding habits, migration, etc. Salim also published other books. His work *'The Fall of Sparrow'* included many incidents from his real life.

Salim not only researched about birds, but also contributed to the arena of protection of nature. For his extraordinary efforts, he was given an international award of INR 5 lakh, but he donated all the money to the Bombay Natural *History Society.* The Government of India honoured him with *Padma Vibushan* in 1983.

This genius man died at the age of 90 on June 20, 1987.

Sheldon Lee Glashow

The American physicist, Sheldon Lee Glashow received the *Nobel Prize for Physics in 1979,* with Steven Weinberg and Abdus Salam for their complementary efforts in originating the *electroweak theory.* This theory is an important contribution to the unification of elementary particles and forces. He is also known for his work which led to the prediction of neutral currents, charmed particles and intermediate vector bosons, all of which were subsequently discovered by experiments. He is the author of around 300 research papers and three books: *Interactions*, *The Charm of Physics,* and *From Alchemy to Quarks*. Currently, he is the *Metcalf Professor of Mathematics and Physics* at the Boston University.

Sheldon Lee Glashow was born on December 5, 1932 in the northern tip of Manhattan in New York City to the Jewish immigrants from Russia. He was the youngest of the three children of Lewis Gluchovsky, a plumber, and Bella Rubin. He received his early education from the Bronx High School of Science in New York City. In 1954, he completed his graduation in Arts from the Cornell University and five years later in 1959, he received a Ph.D. degree in physics from the Harvard University under Nobel-laureate physicist Julian Schwinger. At Harvard, he founded important theories of electromagnetic and nuclear particle interaction, which laid the basis for the next generation of research on quarks and leptons.

Contributions & Achievements:

After a small period at the *Bohr Institute in Copenhagen, CERN* in Geneva, and the *California Institute of Technology, Glashow* spent five years (1961 to 1966) teaching at the University of Stanford and the University of California (Berkeley), before returning to Harvard in 1967 as lecturer of physics. He has served the *science policy committee of CERN* since 1979.

During 1972, Glashow married Joan Alexander, with whom he had two children, Bryan and Rebecca, and two step-children, Jason and Jordan.

With the assistance of Julian Schwinger, Glashow in 1961 extended his work on *electroweak unification models.* Through his works he discovered the basis of the accepted theory of the *electroweak interactions* and was awarded the *Nobel Prize in Physics in 1979,* along with Steven Weinberg and Abdus Salam.

In 1964, while working with James Bjorken, Glashow was the first to predict the existence of a fourth quark, which he originally named the 'charmed quark' (now charm quick). Through this he demonstrated that the quark pairs would largely cancel out flavour changing neutral currents, as well as eliminating a technical disaster for any quantum field theory with unequal numbers of quarks and leptons-an irregularity.

Along with *Howard Georgi in 1973, Glashow devised the first grand unified theory.* This work was the groundwork for all future unifying work.

Apart from scientific articles, Glashow has written a number of popular articles, a collection of tales, charts, cartoons, and poems about physics and physicists. He is also one of the members of *the Board of Sponsors of The Bulletin of the Atomic Scientists. He was the focus of a far-reaching profile in the Atlantic Monthly* during August 1984.

Sigmund Freud

1856 – 1939

Sigmund Freud (May 6, 1856 – September 23, 1939, physiologist, medical doctor, psychologist, was an influential thinker of the 20 century. Freud's innovative treatment of human actions, dreams and indeed of cultural object s as invariably possessing implicit symbolic significance has proven to be extraordinarily productive, and has had immense implications for a wide variety of fields, including anthropology, semiotics and artistic creativity along with appreciation in addition to psychology. However, Freud's most important and frequently reiterated claim, that with psychoanalysis, he had invented a new science of the mind, remains the subject of much disapproval and controversy.

Contributions & Achievements:

Freud conceptualised the mind symbolically as an ancient ruin which had to been uncovered much like an archaeologist would discover the treasures of an ancient civilization. This gave birth to Psychoanalysis. Freud's account of the sexual genesis and nature of neuroses led him naturally to develop a clinical treatment for treating such disorders. This has become so influential today that when people speak of 'psychoanalysis', they frequently refer exclusively to the clinical treatment. The object of psychoanalytic treatment may be said to be a form of self-understanding, once this is acquired, it is largely up to the patient, in consultation with the analyst to determine how he shall handle this newly-acquired understanding of the unconscious forces which motivate him. Freud became more and more sophisticated in his technique of psychoanalysis, and he became particularly adept at using his patient's biased impressions of him to help the patient to discover the origins of the unconscious memory which led to the symptoms from which they suffered.

Freud's theories and research methods have always been controversial. He and psychoanalysis have been criticised in very extreme terms. For an often-quoted example, Peter Medawar, a Nobel Prize winning immunologist, said in 1975 that psychoanalysis is the 'most stupendous intellectual confidence trick of the 20th century'. However, Freud has had a tremendous impact on psychotherapy. Many psychotherapists follow Freud's approach to an extent, even if they reject his theories.

The contemporary scientific climate in which Freud lived and worked should be taken into consideration. When the towering scientific figure of 19th century science, Charles Darwin, published his revolutionary Origin of Species, Freud was four years old. The evolutionary principle completely altered the existing conception of man, whereas, before man had been seen as a being different in nature to the members of the animal kingdom by virtue of his possession of an immortal soul, he was now seen as being part of the natural order, different from non-human animals only in degree of structural difficulty.

This made it possible and reasonable for the first time to treat man as an object of scientific investigation, and to imagine of the vast and varied range of human behaviour, and the motivational causes from which it springs, as being amenable in principle to scientific explanation. Much of the creative work done in a whole variety of diverse scientific fields over the next century was to be inspired by and derive nourishment from this new world-view which Freud, with his enormous esteem for science, accepted implicitly.

Freud also followed Plato in his account of the nature of mental health or psychological well-being, which he saw as the establishment of a melodic relationship between the three elements which constitute the mind. A key concept introduced by Freud was that the mind possesses a number of 'defense mechanisms' to attempt to prevent conflicts from becoming too acute, such as repression (pushing conflicts back into the unconscious), sublimation (channeling the sexual drives into the Achievements socially acceptable goals, in art, science, poetry, etc.), fixation (the failure to progress beyond one of the developmental stages), and regression (a return to the behaviour characteristic of one of the stages).

Published Works:

Freud's work is preserved in a 23 volume set called *The Standard Edition of the Complete Psychological Works of Sigmund Freud.* Some of

Freud's most interesting works are The Interpretation of Dreams, his own favourite, The Psychopathology of Everyday Life, about Freudian slips and other day-to-day oddities, Totem and Taboo, Freud's views on our beginnings, Civilization and Its Discontents, his pessimistic commentary on modern society, and The Future of an Illusion, on religion. All are a part of The Standard Edition, but all are available as separate paperbacks as well. *This renowned man died of cancer of the mouth and jaw that he had been suffering since 20 years of his life.*

Srinivasa Ramanujan

1887-1920

Srinivasa Ramanujan Aiyangar was an *Indian Mathematician* who was born in Erode, India in 1887 on December 22. He was born into a family that was not very well to do. He went to school at the nearby place, Kumbakonam. Ramanujan is very well known for his efforts on continued fractions and series of *hypergeometry*. When Ramanujan was thirteen, he could work out *Loney's Trigonometry* exercises without any help. At the age of fourteen, he was able to acquire the theorems of cosine and sine given by L. Euler. Synopsis of Elementary Results in Pure and Applied Mathematics by George Shoobridge Carr was reached by him in 1903. The book helped him a lot and opened new dimensions to him which helped him introduce about 6,165 theorems for himself. As he had no proper and good books in his reach, he had to figure out on his own the solutions for all the questions. It was in this quest that he discovered many tremendous methods and new algebraic series.

In 1904, he received a merit scholarship in a local college and became more indulgent into mathematics. He lost his interest in all other subjects due to which he lost his scholarship. Even after two attempts, he did not succeed to get a first degree in the field of arts. In 1909, he got married and continued his clerical work and, side by side, his investigations of mathematics. Finally in 1911, he published some of his results.

Contributions & Achievements:

It was in January 1913 that he sent his work to a Cambridge Professor named G. H. Hardy but he did not appreciate Ramanujan's work much as he had not really done to reach the standards of the mathematicians of the West. But he was given a scholarship in May by the *University of Madras (Chennai)*.

Ramanujan went to Cambridge in 1914 and it helped him a lot but by that time his mind worked on the patterns on which it had worked before and he seldom adopted new ways. By then, it was more about intuition than argument. Hardy said Ramanujan could have become an *outstanding mathematician* if his skills had been recognised earlier. It was said about his talents of continued fractions and hypergeometric series that, "he was unquestionably one of the great masters." It was due to his sharp memory, calculative mind, patience and insight that he was a great formalist of his days. But it was due to his some methods of working in the work analysis and theories of numbers that did not let him excel that much.

He got elected as the fellow in 1918 at the Trinity College at Cambridge and the Royal Society. He departed from this world on April 26, 1920.

Stephen Hawking

Born 1942

Stephen Hawking is an English theoretical physicist and cosmologist who is widely considered to be one of the greatest scientists alive today. He is currently the director of research at the *Center for Theoretical Cosmology, University of Cambridge.*

Born on January 8, 1942 to a biologist father, Hawking had two younger sisters. He was an average student at school, deeply interested in science. After winning a scholarship in natural sciences, he acquired a degree in physics from the University College, Oxford. Thereafter, Hawking also studied astronomy and cosmology at the Trinity Hall, Cambridge.

In his early days at Cambridge, Hawking was diagnosed with Amyotrophic Lateral Sclerosis (ALS), a motor neuron disease in which the nerves controlling the muscles become inactive, while the sensory nerves function normally. Due to this sustained condition, it normally takes him about 40 hours to devise a 45 minute lecture.

Contributions & Achievements:

Hawking is known for furthering Einstein's theory of general relativity with quantum theory. He has about *twelve honorary degrees.* Awarded the CBE in 1982, he became a Companion of Honour in 1989. He received numerous awards, medals and praises. Hawking is also a *Fellow of The Royal Society* and a *Member of the US National Academy of Sciences.* He was honoured with the *Presidential Medal of Freedom* in 2009.

Stephen Hawking is working as the Lucasian Professor of Mathematics since 1979, a position once held by Sir Isaac Newton. Arguably, the most famous scientist alive today, he is considered a living legend for his amazing contributions to *quantum physics.*

A highly successful active lecturer and author, Hawking makes use of an adaptive communication system known as *Equalizer* to combat ALS. It involves a speech synthesizer. Using the Equalizer, he has authored a book and several scientific papers and lectures, though he is capable of speaking at a mere rate of 15 words per minute.

Hawking's 1988 book "A Brief History of Time" quickly became an instant best-seller and was translated into 30 languages. It has sold over 10 million copies worldwide to date. His 2001 book "The Universe in a Nutshell" is hailed as a masterpiece in the history of modern physics.

Stephen Hawking got married to Jane Wilde, a language student, in 1965, and together they have three children and one grandchild.

The couple got separated in 1991. As of 2009, Hawking has been almost completely paralysed.

Svante Arrhenius

1859 – 1927

Svante Arrhenius was a Swedish physicist and physical chemist who formulated the theory of electrolytic dissociation. One of the founding fathers of physical chemistry, Arrhenius also present a revolutionary model of the *greenhouse effect.* He won the *1903 Nobel Prize for Chemistry* for his brilliant contributions.

Born on February 19, 1859 near Uppsala, Sweden, Svante Arrhenius's father worked the for Uppsala University as a land surveyor. A childhood prodigy, Arrhenius taught himself to read and even solve simple mathematics problems when he was only three. He received his early education from the renowned Cathedral School in Uppsala. After completing his bachelor's degree in 1878, Arrhenius earned a doctorate in 1884 at the Uppsala University, where he was also awarded the the *honourary title of docent* the same year.

Svante Arrhenius sent his *150-page* thesis regarding the conductivities of electrolytes to several famous scientists across Europe. Wilhelm Ostwald was very much impressed, who even made a trip to Uppsala to recruit Arrhenius for his research team.

Contributions & Achievements:

Arrhenius extensively broadened his ionic theory in 1884 and gave *detailed definitions for acids and bases.* He received a travel stipdend from the *Royal Swedish Academy of Sciences in 1886.* Arrhenius revolutionised the study of electrolytes by stating that electrolytes are separated into ions when there is no current flowing through the solution.

Controversies regarding the causes of the ice ages led Arrhenius to build the earliest climate model of the influence of atmospheric carbon dioxide, which he presented in 'The Philosophical Magazine' in 1896.

He, therefore, became the first scientist to discuss the effect of industrial activity on *global warming*. Arrhenius also performed an extensive research on *bacterial toxins* and *various plant and animal poisons*.

Svante Arrhenius suffered a serious attack of acute intestinal cancer in September 1927. He died a few days later on October 2, 1927. Buried in Uppsala, Arrhenius was 68 years old.

Thabit ibn Qurra

826 - 901

Al-Sabi Thabit ibn Qurra al-Harrani (836 –901) was an astronomer and mathematician born in the present day, Turkey, best known for translating classic Greek works on astronomy, and discovered an equation for determining the amicable numbers. He was a Mandean physician, who was known as Thebit in Latin.

Thabit was a member of the Sabian religious sect. His heritage was sharp in traditions of *Hellenistic culture* and *pagan veneration of the stars.* This background, and in particular his knowledge of Greek and Arabic, made him an attractive prospect for enclosure in one particular community of scholars, the Banu Musa and their circle in Baghdad. Thabit seems to have been asked to join this circle by a family member, the mathematician, Muhammad ibn Musa ibn Shakir, who recognised his talents and potentials.

Thabit subsequently came to fame after travelling to Baghdad when he was invited by Muhammad bin Musa bin Shakir, one of the Banu Musa brothers. He worked in Baghdad and occupied himself with mathematics, astronomy, mechanics, medicine and philosophy.

Contributions & Achievements:

Thabit is credited with dozens of treatises, covering a wide range of fields and topics. While some were written in his native Syriac, most were composed in Arabic. Thabit was trilingual, a skill that enabled him to play a key role in the translation movement of the 9th century Baghdad. He translated works from both Syriac and Greek into Arabic, creating Arabic versions of important *Hellenistic and Greek writings.* Several of Thabit's Arabic translations are the only extant versions of important ancient works.

The medieval astronomical theory of the trepidation of the equinoxes is often attributed to Thabit. He developed a theory about the *trepidation and oscillation of the equinoctial points,* of which many scholars debated in the Middle Ages.

According to Copernicus, Thabit determined the length of the sidereal year as 365 days, 6 hours, 9 minutes and 12 seconds (an error of 2 seconds). Copernicus based his claim on the Latin text attributed to Thabit. Thabit published his observations of the Sun. In the fields of mechanics and physics he may be recognized as the founder of statics. He observed conditions of equilibrium of bodies, beams and levers. Thabit also wrote on philosophical and cosmological topics, questioning some of the fundamentals of the Aristotelian cosmos.

He rejected Aristotle's concept of the *essence as immobile*, a position Rosenfeld and Gregorian suggest is in keeping with his anti Aristotelian stance of allowing the use of motion in mathematics. Thabit also wrote important treatises related to Archimedean problems in statics and mechanics. Besides all these contributions he also founded a school of translation and supervised the translation of a further large number of books from Greek to Arabic.

Among Thabit's writings, a large number have survived, while several are not present. Most of the books are on mathematics, followed by astronomy and medicine. The books have been written in Arabic but some are in Syriac. In the Middle Ages, some of his books were translated into Latin by Gherard of Cremona. In recent centuries, a number of his books have been translated into European languages and published. Thabit's efforts provided a foundation for continuing work in the investigation and reformation of *Ptolemaic astronomy.* His life is illustrative of the fact that individuals from a wide range of backgrounds and religions contributed to the flourishing of sciences like astronomy in Islamic culture.

Thabit died in Baghdad. he and his grandson, *Ibrahim ibn Sinan studied the curves which are needed for making of sundials* that is commendable and is a great source of inspiration for the learners.

Theodor Schwann

Theodor Schwann was a German physiologist who is widely credited as the *founder of modern histology.* He played a vital role in the *development of cell theory* and defined the cell as the *fundamental unit of animal structure.*

Theodor Schwann was born in Neuss, Germany in 1810. His father was a goldsmith. Schwann loved tinkering with mechanical devices as a child. He studied medicine at the universities of Bonn, Würzburg and Berlin.

Schwann completed his graduation in 1834 and accepted a job at a *Berlin anatomy museum.*

Contributions & Achievements:

He discovered *the digestive enzyme, pepsin* during this time. He also researched *fermentation* and *muscle movement* and made i*mportant discoveries.*

He was appointed a professor of anatomy at the University of Leuven, Belgium in 1838. Schwann discovered the organic nature of yeast and also coined the term 'metabolism'.

Schwann implemented *Matthias Schleiden's cell theory* to animals in 1839, and demonstrated that every *mature animal tissue is composed of embryonic cells.*

He later moved to the University of Liège, Belgium in 1848, where he taught physiology and anatomy.

In his later life, Theodor Schwann had developed a passion in *theological issues. Schwann, however, continued to study cells until his death in 1882.* He was 72 years old when he died.

Theodosius Dobzhansky

1900 - 1975

Widely regarded as the founder of *evolutionary genetics, Theodosius Dobzhansky* was an eminent Ukrainian-American geneticist and evolutionist. He played a vital role in the development of evolutionary theory and genetics.

Born in Nemirov, Russian Empire in 1900, Theodosius Dobzhansky was the son of a high school mathematics teacher. He belonged to a family of Russian Orthodox priests. During his childhood, Dobzhansky had developed a passion of collecting insects, and was an ardent fan of outdoor activities. In his high-school days, he decided to become a biologist. After graduating in biology from the University of Kiev in 1921, Dobzhansky accepted a position at the Polytechnic Institute of Kiev on the faculty of agriculture.

Contributions & Achievements:

During his stay as a professor and researcher, Theodosius Dobzhansky started devoting his efforts to the emerging field of genetics. He studied many newer areas of genetics, starting extensive research on the fruit-fly *(Drosophila melanogaster)*. Many contemporary geneticists followed his work, such as Russian entomologist Yuri Filipchenko, who was Dobzhansky's fellow professor at Leningrad University until 1927. He also later analysed the genetics of horses and cattle.

Dobzhansky followed zoologist Thomas Hunt Morgan to the California Institute of Technology in 1928, working as assistant professor in genetics. A few years later, in 1933, he made an important breakthrough when Dobzhansky changed his model organism to *Drosophila pseudoobscura.* The results corroborated his work *'Genetics and the Origin of Species'.* which was published in 1937, and turned out to be the most important book on *evolutionary biology* of the 20th century. A combination of Darwinian selection and modern genetics, it became a catalyst for future researches in evolution.

Dobzhansky joined the *Columbia University* in 1940, making an energetic group of genetics researchers around him. He moved to the *Rockefeller University* in 1962, where he remained until his retirement in 1970. Dobzhansky revolutionised the application of genetics and evolution to the understanding of human beings. He also wrote about *anthropological and philosophical themes*, for instance his influential 1962 work, 'Mankind Evolving', that changed the face of *modern genetics and evolutionary theory.*

Theodosius Dobzhansky retired from the *Rockefeller University* in 1970, and announced to join the University of California at Davis as a supervisor. He died five years later, in 1975, following a *long battle with Leukemia.* He was 75 years old.

Thomas Alva Edison

1847 – 1931

Thomas Alva Edison is one of the greatest American inventors who held countless patents, majority of them related to electricity and power. While two of his most famous inventions are the *incandescent lamp* and the *phonograph*, arguably the most significant invention of Edison is considered to be organised research.

Edison was born on February 11, 1847 in the historic city of Milan (Ohio). His father was a versatile person and a man-of-all-work, while his mother was a teacher. Edison was mostly homeschooled by his mother. Edison became a salesman of fruit, paper and other goods on the Grand Trunk Railroad at a tender age of 12. With the help of his tiny handpress in a trash car, he wrote and published the *Grand Trunk Herald* in 1862, which was sent to 400 railroad employees. The same year Edison worked as a telegraph operator, trained by the father of a kid whose life he had saved. Edison was a *tramp telegrapher,* as he was exempted from military service due to his deafness. He was recruited in 1868 by the *Western Union Telegraph Company* in Boston.

Contributions & Achievements:

Early Conceptions:

Perhaps, the first invention of Edison was a *telegraph repeater* in 1864 which worked automatically, while his earliest patent was registered for an electric vote recorder. He acquired partnership in a New York electrical company in 1869, where he honed the stock ticker and sold it. With all his money, Edison paid for his own factory in Newark, N.J., where he hired technicians to help him, with the inventions. His dream was to create an 'invention factory.' Almost 80 'earnest men,' including physicists, mathematicians and chemists, were among his collaborators. 'Invention to order' made him good money at this place.

From 1870 to 1875, Edison devised many telegraphic advances including receivers, transmitters, the duplex, tape and automatic printers. He also collaborated in 1871 with Christopher Sholes, also known as 'father of the typewriter', to ameliorate the typing machine. Edison claimed to have made twelve typewriters at Newark in 1870. As a result, the Remington Company purchased his interests.

Edison's carbon telegraph transmitter for Western Union brought a breakthrough for the creation of the Bell telephone. The money he got from Western Union for the transmitter was spent to establish a factory in Menlo Park, N.J. One more time, he used scientific talent to register over 300 patents in only 6 years. *His electric pen (1877) developed stencils to produce copies.*

Other Inventions and Contributions:

Probably, his most impressive invention, the *phonograph*, was patented in 1877. By 1890, Edison had about 80 patents under his name, and that was pretty much the reason, *The Victor Company* came into being.

To explore *incandescence*, Edison and his fellows, among them *J. P. Morgan,* developed the *Edison Electric Light Company* in 1878. Years later, the company became the *General Electric Company.* Edison invented the first practical incandescent lamp in 1879. With months of hard work researching metal filaments, Edison and his staff analyzed 6,000 organic fibres around the world and determined that the *Japanese bamboo* was ideal for mass production. Large-scale production of these *cheap lamps* turned out to be profitable, hence the first *fluorescent lamp* was patented in 1896.

Edison made an amazing discovery in pure science, termed as the *Edison Effect*. He discovered in 1883 that *electrons flowed from incandescent filaments.* The lamp could function as a valve using a metal-plate insert, while taking only negative electricity. A method to transmit telegraphic 'aerial' signals over short distances was patented by Edison in 1885. The 'wireless' patent was later sold to *Guglielmo Marconi.*

The huge West Orange, N.J. factory was supervised from 1887 to 1931 by Edison. This was probably the world's most cutting-edge research laboratory, and a forerunner to modern research and development laboratories, with experts systematically investigating and researching for the solution of problems.

The Edison battery, made perfect in 1910, used an alkaline electrolyte, and proved to be a superb storage device. The copper oxide battery, strikingly similar to modern dry cells, was modified in 1902.

The kinetograph, his motion picture camera, was able to photograph action on 50-foot strips of film, and produced about 16 images per foot. A young assistant of Edison built a small laboratory in 1893 called the 'Black Maria,' which was substantial in making the first Edison movies. The *kinetoscope projector of 1893 finally displayed the films.* The earliest commercial movie theater a peepshow, was established in New York in 1884. After developing and modifying the projector of Thomas Armat in 1895, Edison commercialized it as the 'Vitascope'.

The *Edison Company* created over *1,700 movies.* Edison set the benchmark for *talking pictures* in 1904 by synchronising movies with the *phonograph.* His cinemaphone adjusted the film speed to phonograph speed. The kinetophone projected talking pictures in 1913. The phonograph, behind the screen, was synchronised by pulleys and ropes with the projector. Edison brought forth many 'talkies.'

The universal motor, which utilised alternating or direct current, appeared in 1907. The electric safety lantern, patented in 1914, significantly reduced casualties among miners. The same year, Edison devised the *telescribe*, which unified characteristics of the telephone and the *dictating phonograph.*

Services for the Government:

Edison presided the U.S. Navy Consulting Board throughout World War I and made 45 more inventions. These inventions included substitutes for antecedently imported chemicals (such as carbolic acid), a ship-telephone system, an underwater searchlight, defensive instruments against U-boats, among others. Later on, Edison launched the *Naval Research Laboratory,* the eminent American institution for research involving organized weapons.

This multi-genius died on Oct. 18, 1931 in West Orange, N.J. The laboratory buildings and equipments affiliated with Edison were upheld in Greenfield Village, Detroit and Michigan by Henry Ford, a friend and admirer.

Thomas Hunt Morgan

1866 – 1945

Thomas Hunt Morgan was an eminent American zoologist and geneticist. He is known for his *legendary experimental analysis of the fruit fly,* after which he formulated the *chromosome theory of heredity*. Morgan also demonstrated that genes are *connected in a series on chromosomes,* which carry hereditary traits, therefore kick starting the modern field of genetics.

He won the *1933 Nobel Prize for Physiology or Medicine* for his extraordinary Achievementss.

Born in Lexington, Kentucky, on September 25, 1866 to a rich, influential southern family, Thomas Hunt Morgan earned his *B.S. degree* from the *State College of Kentucky* (now the University of Kentucky) in 1886, and his Ph.D. degree from the Johns Hopkins University in 1890. After his doctorate, Morgan joined the faculty of Bryn Mawr College for a while.

Contributions & Achievements:

Thomas Hunt Morgan was appointed a professor of experimental zoology at the Columbia University in 1904. He established a large laboratory at this place that was later termed as the 'Fly Room.' In collaboration with fellow biologist Lilian Morgan and several other assistants, Morgan studied and highlighted the two specific characteristics of the fruit fly (*Drosophila melanogaster*). They were able to demonstrate the results of mating individual flies having these specific characteristics. The discovery is regarded as the earliest to extend *Mendel's genetics* from the plants into the animals.

Morgan also extensively studied the field of *experimental embryology*. He knew the hypothetical connections between genetics and development, but was rather unwilling at the time to reveal those links explicitly.

Morgan won the *1924 Darwin Medal*, the *1933 Nobel Prize* for *Physiology* or *Medicine* and the *1939 Copley Medal.*

Thomas Hunt Morgan continued to work in the laboratory until his death. He died in Pasadena, California, of a heart failure on December 4, 1945. Morgan was 79 years old.

Thomas Newcomen

Thomas Newcomen was a prominent British engineer, best known for inventing the *atmospheric steam* engine, which was the world's, oldest known steam engine for pumping water. The Newcomen engine largely influenced later designs, such as the *James Watt's engine.*

Born in Dartmouth, Devon, England, Thomas Newcomen initially worked as an ironmonger at Dartmouth. Since flooding was a major problem in the area, Newcomen, with the help of a plumber named John Calley, extensively worked on a steam pump, which was found to be much efficient than Thomas Savery's conventional crude pump.

Contributions & Achievements:

In this design, the intensity of pressure was not restricted by the pressure of the steam. Newcomen devised the internal-condensing jet for producing a vacuum in the cylinder and an automatic valve gear.

The first operational Newcomen engine was built in 1712 near Dudley Castle, Staffordshire. It proved to be a very efficient and cost-effective tool for drainage of mines and raising water to power waterwheels.

Thomas Newcomen died on August 5, 1729 in London, England. He was 65 years old.

Tycho Brahe

Tyge Ottesen Brahe, more commonly known as *Tycho Brahe* (latinised form), was an eminent Danish astronomer and alchemist. He played a vital role in the *development of various astronomical instruments.* Brahe is also known for his *precise and comprehensive astronomical and planetary observations,* which heavily influenced future discoveries.

Born at Knutstorp Castle, Scania in 1546, Tycho Brahe was raised in an influential and noble Danish family. He received his early education in a Latin school.

Brahe entered the *University of Copenhagen when he was only 12.* After initially studying law, he soon gained an interest in *astronomy*, having witnessed a *great solar eclipse* when he was 13 years old. Tycho later attended the Universities of Rostock and Basel.

Contributions & Achievements:

The brilliant astronomical observations of Tycho Brahe were highly influential to the scientific revolution. He made amazingly accurate and precise astronomical observations for his times, even without the help of the telescope.

Brahe was an active participant to the debates on the nature of the Universe. Although better known as a famed astronomer, Tycho Brahe also played a crucial role in the development of *geodesy and cartography.*

Instruments built by Brahe proved to be very helpful in accurate determinations of latitudes and longitudes. His groundbreaking *contributions to the lunar theory was his renowned discovery of the variation of the Moon's longitude.*

The maps of Hven drawn by Brahe were one of the earliest in the whole of Scandinavia to use systematic triangulation.

Tycho Brahe died on October 24, 1601 in Prague, Czechia, supposedly due to bladder complications. He was 54 years old.

Virginia Apgar

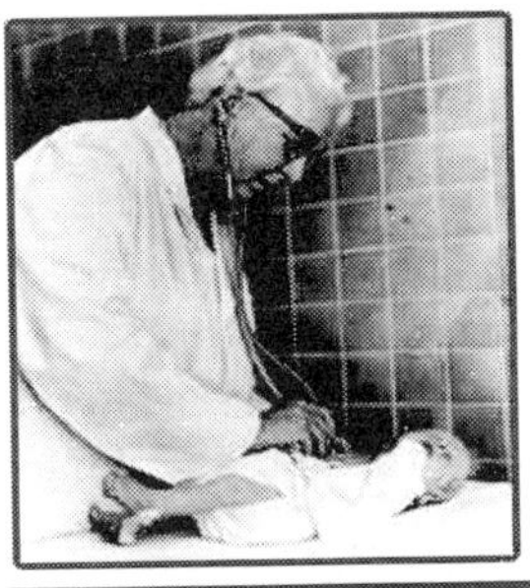

1909 – 1974

The American physician, Virginia Apgar is best known for developing the *Apgar Newborn Scoring System* (better known as the 'Apgar Score'), a simple, quick method for judging newborn viability. The newborn's appearance colour, reflex irritability, muscle tone and respiration are assessed one minute and five minutes after birth; low scores indicate possible health issues. The test has saved countless infants, laid the foundations of neonatology and caught potentially grave conditions. She was one of the Columbia University's first female M.D.s and one of the first American women to specialise in anesthesia.

Apgar was born on June 7, 1909 in Westfield, New Jersey. Belonging to a family of amateur musicians, Apgar enjoyed playing violin and other instruments, and became a skilled musician.

Contributions & Achievements:

A Mount Holyoke graduate, Apgar was one of a few women to complete her graduation during the 1930s from the *Columbia's College of Physicians and Surgeons (1933)*. In 1937, she successfully completed a residency in surgery at Columbia. However, she was dejected from practising surgery by Dr. Allen Whipple, the chair of surgery at Columbia. She finished her training in anesthesia and returned to Columbia in 1938 as director of the newly formed division of anesthesia. In 1938, she accepted the position of the director of anesthesiology at Columbia-Presbyterian Medical Center-the university's first female department head. Also, she became Columbia's College of Physicians and Surgeons first professor of anesthesiology in 1949 (a post which she held until 1959), while, she also did clinical and research work at the affiliated Sloane Hospital for Women.

In 1949, Virginia Apgar came up with the *Apgar Score System* (presented in 1952 and published in 1953), which became popular in the United States and elsewhere. Before her discovery, babies at birth were assumed to be in good health unless they exhibited some obvious suffering or imperfection: needless to say, internal deficiencies (e.g., circulators or respiratory) could be missed, resulting all too often in death. Because Apgar realised that "Birth is the most hazardous time of life," she designed a system for quickly and accurately assessing a baby's health in the crucial minutes after birth. While examining the system's effectiveness, Apgar found out that cyclopropane as an anesthetic for the mother had a harmful effect on the infant, and due to which, its use in labour was put to an end.

In 1959, Apgar obtained a master's degree in public health from Johns Hopkins and also the executive position with the March of Dimes. In that capacity, she worked hard to improve the healthcare of infants and children. For the next 14 years, until her death, Apgar served as an activist, fund-raiser and an instructor. In 1995, she was introduced into the *National Women's Hall of Fame.*

Agpar published 60 scientific papers. Her book, *Is My Baby All Right?* (1972), co-written with Joan Beck became a popular parenting hardback.

Virginia Apgar died as an unmarried lady on August 7, 1974, at the Columbia-Presbyterian Medical Center. The *Virginia Apgar Award* is given every year by the *American Academy of Pediatrics* for stupendous contributions to the field of *perinatal pediatrics.*

Werner Heisenberg

1901 – 1976

Werner Heisenberg was a *German physicist and philosopher* who is noted for his crucial contributions to *quantum mechanics.* He devised a method to formulate the *quantum mechanics in terms of matrices*, for which he was awarded the *1932 Nobel Prize for Physics.* Heisenberg is widely considered as one of the most influential figures in *nuclear physics, particle physics* and *quantum field theory.*

Born in Würzburg, Germany in 1901, Werner Heisenberg's father was a prominent secondary school teacher. Heisenberg went to the Ludwig-Maximilians-Universität München and the Georg-August-Universität Göttingen, where he studied physics and mathematics from 1920 to 1923. He earned his doctorate in 1923.

Werner Heisenberg ranks alongside Niels Bohr, Paul Dirac and Richard Feynman as far as his influence on contemporary physics is concerned. He was one of the most important figures in the development of *quantum mechanics,* and its modern interpretation.

Contributions & Achievements:

Heisenberg formulated the *quantum theory of ferromagnetism, the neutron-proton model of the nucleus,* the *S-matrix theory in particle scattering,* and various other significant *breakthroughs in quantum field theory* and *high-energy particle physics* are associated with him. As a prolific author, Heisenberg wrote more than 600 original research papers, philosophical essays and explanations for general audiences. His work is still available in the nine volumes of the 'Gesammelte Werke' *(Collected Works).*

Heisenberg is synonymous with the so-called uncertainty, or *indeterminacy, principle of 1927,* for one of the earliest breakthroughs to quantum mechanics in 1925, and for his suggestions of a unified field theory, the so-called 'world formula'. He won the *Nobel Prize for Physics in 1932* at the young age of 31.

Heisenberg stayed firmly in Germany during the worst years of the *Hitler regime,* heading Germany's research efforts on the applications of nuclear fission during World War II. He also played a vital role in the reconstruction of West German Science after the war. Heisenberg's role was crucial in the success of West Germany's nuclear and high-energy physics research programs.

In his later years, Werner Heisenberg assumed various influential positions in Germany and abroad, giving important lectures on *theoretical physics and other subjects.* He died of cancer of the kidneys and gall bladder on February 1, 1976. Heisenberg was 74 years old.

Wilbur and Orville Wright

Wilbur and Orville Wright

1867 - 1912
1871 - 1948

Wilbur and Orville Wright established a marvellous legacy in the history of world, alongside the greatest American inventors, with the invention of the first successful, fully powered and *heavier-than-air flying machine.* The airplane, which was created in Dayton, Ohio and made operational at Kitty Hawk, North Carolina, on December 17, 1903, virtually kicked off the aerial age. The invention is considered as one of the most important events in the 20th century.

The Wright brothers belonged to the deep mid-western America. Various generations on both sides of the family had been erstwhile colonists on the Ohio and Indiana frontier. Milton Wright, the dad, was an itinerant minister, who served as a bishop in the Church of the United Brethren in Christ. His job meant that the family saw many church posts across the place. Susan, the mom, had been a member of the United Brethren, an intelligent and shy person.

Contributions & Achievements:

The Wright Brothers began experimenting in *aeronautics in 1899* as they mastered their skills by 1905. In these six years, with brilliant originality, they determined the necessary elements of the problem, conceptualised creative technical solutions and created practical mechanical design tools with constituents that resulted in an *executable aircraft.* The efforts meant much more than merely coaxing a machine off the ground.

They laid down the *fundamental principles of aircraft design* that are still relevant to this day. After introducing the invention to the public in the United States and Europe in 1908, they gained international fame and recognition. The Wright Company started manufacturing airplanes for sale and created wealth that far exceeded anybody's imaginations.

The contemporary experimenters and aviators responsively overtook and surpassed their designs, but it was Wilbur and Orville Wright who made the landmark discovery that made them immortal in history.

Air transportation and military aviation have had an indeterminable economic, geopolitical and cultural impact in the entire world.

The Wright brothers never got married. Wilbur Wright died of typhoid. He was only 45 years old. Orville Wright died of a heart attack at 77.

Wilhelm Conrad Roentgen

Wilhelm Conrad Röntgen (a.k.a., Roentgen) (1845-1923), the first *Nobel Prize winner in Physics,* was the first to produce *X-rays,* known originally as *Röntgen rays.* The facts of his early biography offer hope for those who fail in their initial educational efforts. A childhood act of solidarity excluded him from many subsequent schools. However, he went on not only to complete his education but to achieve a full professorship. His discovery of the effect of the invisible but powerful rays that revealed the bones inside bodies has made possible *many elements of modern medicine.*

Wilhelm Conrad Röentgen was the child of a Dutch mother and a German father. Although born in Germany, his family, which was Catholic moved to Holland, which is largely Protestant. As a teenager, he made the judgement error of refusing to squeal on a schoolmate who had drawn a rude picture of an instructor. This act of defiance caused his expulsion and his exclusion from other gymnasia, not only in the Netherlands but in his father's nation of Germany as well.

Contributions & Achievements:

Somehow in spite of universal blacklisting, he managed to gain admission to the Federal Polytechnic Institute in Zurich, Switzerland, by an entry exam. He studied mechanical engineering, and went on to the University of Zurich for his PhD. He went on to teach physics at a number of universities. He even considered an offer from the Columbia University, an institution with a history of offering lecterns to brilliant émigrés. However, World War I broke out and he ended up remaining in Munich for the remainder of his professional career.

For decades, he had been studying the effects of electrical charge on the response and appearance of vacuum tubes. The science of electricity was still relatively new, and there remained much to understand. His set-ups used relatively simple components by today's standards.

He conducted a series of experiments in 1895 in which he connected a type of vacuum tube (visualise a light bulb on steroids) called a *Hittorf-Crookes* tube to an early and very powerful *electrostatic charge generator* known as a *Ruhmkorff coil,* similar to what sparks a car motor to start. He was trying to reproduce a fluorescent effect observed with another type of vacuum tube called a *Lenard tube.* The filament inside produced a stream of electrons which was well-known, called a *cathode ray.* To his surprise, this produced fluorescence on a screen coated with a compound called *barium platinocyanide,* several feet away. This suggested to him that a hitherto unknown, and entirely invisible, effect was being produced. We know now that the cathode ray had excited the atoms of the aluminum to produce X-rays, which in turn excited the atoms of the barium (an element which fluoresces readily)

He also discovered that when his hand passed between the electrically charged *vacuum tube and the barium platinocyanide coated screen, he saw his bones. He reproduced this phenomenon with his wife, causing horror.*

After secretly confirming his findings, he published an article titled, *'On A New Kind Of Rays'* (Über eine neue Art von Strahlen). This revelation and its nearly immediate application to all sorts of medical imaging earned him an honorary medical degree. *His Nobel Prize was awarded in 1901.*

Unlike the bios of some other radiation pioneers, his does not end with him giving his life for his seminal work, since he used *lead shielding*. He did, however, die of *intestinal carcinoma.*

Wilhelm Ostwald

1853 – 1932

Friedrich Wilhelm Ostwald, more commonly known as Wilhelm Ostwald, was an eminent Russian-German chemist and philosopher who was a key figure in the *development of physical chemistry* as a recognised branch of chemistry. He won the *1909 Nobel Prize* for Chemistry for his groundbreaking research on chemical equilibria, chemical reaction velocities and catalysis.

Born of German parents in Riga, Latvia in 1853, Wilhelm Ostwald received his early education at the city's Realgymnasium, where he studied physics, chemistry, mathematics and natural history, while learning various languages, such as French, English, Latin and Russian. His father wanted him to become an engineer but Ostwald had already developed an interest in chemistry.

After entering the Dorpat Landesuniversitiit in 1872, Ostwald studied physics under Arthur von Oettingen and chemistry under Karl Schmidt and Johann Lemberg. He received his Candidat in 1875, after writing an essay on the mass action of water. Oettingen consequently took him in as a helper in the physical laboratory. Ostwald received his master's degree after analysing the chemical affinity by physical means. He began to give lectures on physical chemistry at the University, and continued his research on affinity, while refining the scientific methods related to the process.

Ostwald earned a doctorate in 1878 and became Schmidt's assistant in 1879.

Contributions & Achievements:

Wilhelm Ostwald came back to Riga in 1881 to join the Polytechnicum as the Professor of Chemistry, where he soon became a popular teacher and a creative researcher. He worked on two projects that gained him worldwide acclaim; "Lehrbuch Der Allgemeinen Chemie" and "Zeitschrift für Physikalische Chemie". His works massively promoted the growing field of physical chemistry.

Ostwald went to Leipzig in 1887, where he assumed the chair of physical chemistry. There he carried out groundbreaking research on catalysis, while promoting the works of Arrhenius and Van't Hoff. He made Leipzig a world centre for the study of physical chemistry. Moreover, he extensively studied and made important findings regarding energetics. Ostwald spent almost two decades at Leipzig.

Wilhelm Ostwald went into semi-retirement in 1894, choosing to continue only as a research professor. He started focussing more towards 'Naturphilosophie' and kept himself away from research in chemistry. He finally announced full retirement in 1906 and moved to his estate at Grossbothen, in Saxony, where he spent his later years as an independent scholar and freethinker, exploring the fields of energetics, scientific methodology, monism and pacifism and internationalism. He also developed a new *physical theory of colours.*

In 1909, he won the Nobel Prize in chemistry.

Ostwald died at 'Landhans Energie' in 1932, after a short illness. He was 78 years old.

Wilhelm Röntgen

1845 – 1923

The German physicist, Wilhelm Conrad Röntgen was the first person to systematically produce and detect electromagnetic radiation in a wavelength range today known as *x-rays* or *Röntgen rays*. His discovery of x-rays was a great revolution in the fields of physics and medicine and electrified the general public. It also earned him the *Rumford Medal* of the *Royal Society of London* in 1896 and the *first Nobel Prize in Physics in 1901*. He is also known for his discoveries in Mechanics, Heat, and Electricity.

Röntgen was born on March 27, 1845, at Lennep in the Lower Rhine Province of Germany. He was the only child of a merchant and cloth manufacturer. Röntgen was brought up in Netherlands after he and his family moved to Apeldoorn in 1848. Here he first received his early education at the Institute of Martinus Herman van Doorn, a boarding school and in 1861, attended the Utrecht Technical School. Unfortunately in 1863, he was expelled unfairly from his school after being accused of a prank another student had committed. Even though Röntgen did not seem to be especially gifted in his schoolwork, he was good at building mechanical objects, a talent that enabled him to build many of his own experimental devices in his later life.

Contributions & Achievements:

He then entered the University of Utrecht in 1865 to study physics without having the necessary credentials required for a regular student. In 1869, he earned a Ph.D. in mechanical engineering from the University of Zurich. Here he attended lectures by the noted physicist, Rudolf Julius Emmanuel Clausius and also worked in the laboratory of Kundt. As soon as he completed his graduation, he was appointed assistant to Kundt and went with him to Würzburg in the same year, and three years later to

Strasbourg.

In 1874, he was appointed as a lecturer at Strasbourg University and in 1875 served as a professor in the Academy of Agriculture at Hohenheim in Württemberg. In 1876, he returned to Strasbourg as Professor of Physics. Three years later, he accepted the invitation to the Chair of Physics in the University of Giessen. In 1888, he obtained the same position at the University of Würzburg, and in 1900 at the University of Munich. Even though he accepted an appointment at the Columbia University in New York City but due to the occurrence of the World War I, Röntgen changed his plans and remained in Munich for the rest of his career.

Discovery of X-rays:

During 1895, Röntgen carried out his investigations on the phenomenon of Cathode Rays. Accidentally, he put a piece of cardboard covered with fluorescent mineral near the experimental set and noticed it glowing in the dark when the source of cathode rays was turned on. Roentgen immediately initiated an experiment aimed at investigation of the phenomenon.

He found that if vacuum tube, used for experiments with cathode rays, was covered tightly with thin, black cardboard and placed in a darkened room, bright glow was observed during each discharge on a screen covered with fluorescent barium platinum cyanide (placed near the device). He realised that the fluorescence was caused by an agent which could infiltrate from within the vacuum tube through dark cardboard (impermeable to visible or ultraviolet radiation) to the outside of the set. He termed this agent as X-rays.

Röntgen died at Munich on February 10, 1923, from carcinoma of the intestine.

Wilhelm Wundt

1832 - 1920

Wilhelm Wundt was a German physiologist and psychologist, who is widely credited as the founder of *experimental psychology.* Wundt is also acknowledged as one of the greatest and most influential psychologists of all time.

Born at Neckarau, Baden in 1832, Wilhelm Wundt was the son of a Lutheran minister. Wundt received a medical degree at the University of Heidelberg in 1856. He also attended the Universities of Tübingen and Berlin.

After teaching physiology at the University of Heidelberg, Wilhelm Wundt joined Hermann von Helmholtz as an assistant in 1858. During this time, he wrote, 'Beiträge zur Theorie der Sinneswahrnehmung' (Contributions to the Theory of Sense Perception). As one of the early pioneers of scientific psychology, Wundt introduced the usage of experimental methods in psychology, therefore minimising the role of *rational analysis.*

Contributions & Achievements:

After succeeding Helmholtz, he investigated the immediate experiences of consciousness, such as sensations, ideas and feelings, and wrote, 'Grundzüge der physiologischen Psychologie' (Principles of Physiological Psychology), which still remains one of the most influential works in the history of psychology. It also explored the fundamental concepts related to apperception (conscious perception) and introspection (conscious examination of conscious experience).

During his tenure as professor at the University of Leipzig in 1879, Wundt built the first psychological laboratory ever. He also published the first journal of psychology, 'Philosophische Studien' (Philosophical

Studies) in 1881. Some of his later works also included 'Grundriss der Psychologie' (1896) and 'Völkerpsychologie' (1900–20).

Wilhelm Wundt died on August 31, 1920 in Grossbothen, Germany. He was 88 years old.

Willard Frank Libby

Willard Frank Libby (1908-1980), a Nobel Prize Laureate and Guggenheim Fellowship recipient was a pioneer in the use of *differential decay of the Carbon 14 Isotope* for dating organic materials; what we now call *radiocarbon dating.* He *addressed this scientific puzzle* after developing a gaseous diffusion enrichment process for Uranium-235. His work also involved the identification, separation and control of 'heavy water' containing *deuterium* and *tritium*, both *isotopes of Hydrogen.* These processes were important to the *building of the Hiroshima bomb.* Through his post-war appointment to *the Atomic Energy Commission,* he embraced the cause of peaceful nuclear use.

Contributions & Achievements:

War:

His be began in Colorado. He studied chemistry at Berkeley, teaching there until 1941. He worked initially to develop Geiger counters for the detection of background radiation from soils and rock formations; what homeowners call *radon gas.* His Guggenheim post-doctoral fellowship took him to Princeton, but with the outbreak of WW II hostilities, he was recruited into the Manhattan Project at the Columbia University, a massive mobilization of top scientists to develop an atomic weapon. Libby's biography must record his innovation in techniques used to separate and concentrate *uranium isotopes* through *gaseous diffusion.*

Peace:

Post-war, he taught at the Enrico Fermi Institute at the University of Chicago. He made the connection between the amounts of tritium, an unstable isotope of Hydrogen, in water, and the action of cosmic ray bombardment in the highest levels of the atmosphere. Only trace quantities of tritium are found in any body of water, but once the water is isolated from the atmosphere, it no longer acquires *new tritium molecules.* This observation led to pioneering techniques for dating water bodies, and identifying different currents of water in the ocean.

This line of research also led him to discover that the bodies of all organisms, whether plant or animal, absorbed trace amounts of the Carbon 14 isotope only during life. He reasoned that the steady radioactive decay of this other unstable isotope could provide a way to measure the time elapsed since death. The technique of documenting the *degree of decay of the Carbon isotope, C14*, in dead tissues, immediately proved useful. This technology has been immensely helpful to many branches of science, especially *archeology and paleontology.* Its value to science was recognised in the *Nobel Prize he received in 1960.*

Libby believed fully in the possibilities and promises of atomic science, and carried this message for the Eisenhower administration into the media and on the lecture circuit. Libby's advocacy for atoms for peace, while with the Atomic Energy Commission did, however, put him publicly at odds with some other noted scientists, for example, Linus Pauling, who believed that all testings should cease immediately.

Libby put his belief in the survivability of nuclear attack into practice in the construction of his home fallout shelter, which famously burnt immediately upon completion. His enthusiasm occasionally could lead to nearly laughable missteps; for example, he counselled the residents of a rural town with one solitary through-road to flee to the countryside in case of an attack. Since this course of action would have been a virtual guarantee of traffic gridlock, and starvation or dehydration would unavoidably await anyone attempting this strategy, his audience took his advice with the proverbial grain of salt.

No such silliness detracts from the facts of his contribution to every discipline that deals with time – *radiocarbon dating* assures him a place in the *Pantheon of the Greats.*

William Harvey

1578 - 1657

The man who first correctly explained the *process of blood circulation in our bodies and the role of heart in the process* is none other than William Harvey, an *English physician.* He is also known as the *father of modern physiology.*

William Harvey was born on April 1, 1578 in Folkestone, Kent, England, the eldest of seven sons. His father, Thomas Harvey was a jurat of Folkestone. After completing his schooling from the King's School, Canterbury, he joined the Caius College, Cambridge at the age of sixteen. There he studied arts and medicine and received his Bachelor of Arts degree in 1597. His fascination for medicine led him to Italy to study at the University of Padua, the centre for western European medical instruction. Here he studied under the famous anatomist, Fabricius, Julius Casserius, and other renowned men and graduated with honours in 1602. In the same year, he returned to England where he earned yet another medical degree from the Cambridge University. Following this, Harvey established himself in London, joining the College of Physicians on October 5, 1604. The same year, he also got married to Elizabeth Browne, daughter of Lancelot Browne, physician to King James I. They had no children.

Contributions & Achievements:

In 1609, he was chosen a physician to St. Bartholomew's Hospital, and in 1615, Lumleian Lecturer at the College of Physicians – a position that he held for his entire life. His thoughts about circulation of the blood were first publicly expressed in these lectures during 1616. Harvey continued to contribute to the *Lumleain lectures* at the same time also taking care of his patients at St. Bartholomew's Hospital; he thus soon attained an important and fairly lucrative practice, which made possible his appointment as court physician to King James I in 1618 and then to Charles I in 1625, a post he held until Charles was beheaded in 1649. Charles helped Harvey by providing him with deer from the royal parks for his medical research. Harvey stood firm with Charles, looking after him even during the *Cromwellian Civil War,* which led to the sacking of Harvey's rooms in 1642 and the demolition of many of his medical notes and papers. He stopped working at the end of the Civil War, a widower, and lived with his various brothers.

Harvey's discovery of the circulation of blood is considered as his greatest contribution to the field of medicine. His many experimental dissections and vivisections made him reject Galen's views about blood movement, particularly the concepts that blood was formed in the liver and absorbed by the body, and that it flowed through the septum (dividing wall) of the heart. Harvey first examined the heartbeat, finding the existence of the pulmonary circulation and noting the one-way flow of blood. In his attempt to discover the amount of blood pumped by the heart, he figured out that there must be a constant amount of blood flowing through the arteries and returning through the veins of the heart, following a cycle. He presented this explanation in 1628 in his publication -*An Anatomical Study of the Motion of the Heart and of the Blood in Animals.*

He published another ground-breaking book in 1651 titled as 'Essays on the Generation of Animals.' This book is considered the basis for modern embryology.

This great physician died of a stroke at the age of 79, on June 3, 1657 at Roehampton. He is buried in Hempstead church.

William Herschel

1738 - 1822

Sir William Herschel was a German-born British astronomer and composer, who is widely credited as the founder of *sidereal astronomy for observing the heavenly bodies*. He found the planet, Uranus and its two moons, and formulated a *theory of stellar evolution*. Knighted in 1816, Herschel was also the first astronomer to suggest that *nebulae are composed of stars*.

Born in Hanover, Brunswick-Lüneburg on November15, 1738, William Herschel's father was a musician who worked for German Army. Following the French invasion of Hanover in 1757, his father sent him to seek refuge in England, where Herschel became a music teacher and composer.

After studying Robert Smith's 'Harmonics' and 'A Compleat System of Opticks', William Herschel soon developed an interest in the techniques of telescope construction, as well as the distant celestial bodies. He built his own telescope and eyepieces that were advanced enough to have a magnifying power of 6,450 times. Herschel conducted two preliminary telescopic surveys of the heavens, and in 1781, during his third survey of the night sky, he discovered an extraordinary object, which was actually the planet *Uranus*, and its two moons, *Titania and Oberon.*

Contributions & Achievements:

The discovery earned him the *Copley Medal* and a fellowship at the *Royal Society of London.*

Herschel later studied the *nature of nebulae* and discovered that all nebulae were formed of stars, hence, *rejecting the long-held belief that nebulae were composed of a luminous fluid.* He also discovered two *moons of Saturn,* namely *Mimas and Enceladus,* and coined the term, 'asteroid'. Herschel maintained that the Solar System is moving through space and found out the direction of that movement. He also suggested that the Milky Way was in the shape of a disk.

William Herschel was appointed a *foreign member of the Royal Swedish Academy of Sciences in 1813,* and was knighted three years later in 1816. He died on August 25, 1822 in Slough, Berkshire. Herschel was 83 years old.

William Thomson

1824-1907

William Thomson was born in Belfast, Ireland June 26, 1824 at Baron Kelvin of Largs. William attended the *Glasgow University* from the age of 10. This early age is not quite as unusual as one would think, for at that time, the universities in Scotland to some extent competed with the schools for the most able junior pupils. William Thomson graduated from Glasgow and Cambridge showing precocious ability in Mathematics and Physics. *He became professor of Natural Philosophy at Glasgow at a very young age*.

Having studied some of Thomson's research contributions, let us comment on the innovations he introduced into teaching at the University of Glasgow. He introduced laboratory work into the degree courses, keeping this part of the work distinct from the mathematical side.

Another of Thomson's famous pieces of work was his joint project with Tait to produce their famous *Text Treatise on Natural Philosophy,* which they began working on in the early 1860s. They worked by posting a notebook back and forward to each other on this huge project which Thomson envisioned as covering all physical theories.

Contributions & Achievements:

Thomson achieved his greatest fame through an event that we have still to discuss. He was always greatly interested in the improvement of physical instrumentation, and Thomson designed and implemented many new devices, including the mirror-galvanometer that was used in the first successful sustained telegraph transmissions in transatlantic submarine cable.

He was created 'Lord Kelvin' for his work on the *first transatlantic cable*. Thomson had joined a *group of industrialists in the mid 1850s* on a project to lay a *submarine* cable between *Ireland and Newfoundland.*

He played several roles in this project, being on the board of directors and also being an advisor on *theoretical electrical matters.*

He helped develop the *second law of thermodynamics* but Kelvin argued that the key issue in the interpretation of the Second Law of Thermodynamics was the explanation of irreversible processes.

He noted that if entropy always increased, the universe would ultimately reach a state of uniform temperature and maximum entropy from which it would not be possible to extract any work. He called this the *Heat Death of the Universe.* Therefore, he proposed a *thermodynamical theory* based on the dominance of the energy concept, on which he believed all physics should be based.

He said the *two laws of thermodynamics* expressed the *indestructibility and dissipation of energy.* By 1847, Thomson had already gained a good reputation as a scientist when he attended the *British Association for the Advancement of Science annual meeting in Oxford* where he stated "There is nothing new to be discovered in physics now. All that remains is more and more precise measurement."

At that meeting, he heard *James Prescott Joule argue for the mutual convertibility of heat and mechanical work* and for their mechanical *equivalence.* In 1848, he provided only an operational definition of temperature.

He proposed an *absolute temperature scale in which a unit of heat* descending from a body A to a body B at the same temperature would give out the same mechanical effect, whatever be the number. Such a scale would be quite independent of the physical properties of any specific substance. In his publication, Thomson wrote:

"The conversion of heat (or caloric) into mechanical effect is probably impossible, certainly undiscovered."

One of the clearest instances of *this interaction is in his estimate* of *the age of the Earth.* Given his youthful work on the figure of the Earth and his interest in heat conduction, it is no surprise that he chose to investigate the Earth's cooling and to make historical inferences of the Earth's age from his calculations.

Thomson was a creationist in a broad sense, but he was not a 'flood geologist'. He contended that the *laws of thermodynamics* operated from the birth of the universe and envisaged a dynamic process that saw the organisation and evolution of the solar system and other structures, followed by a gradual heat death.

Thomson was also a *yachtsman*, as he was a lot interested in the *sea related stuff.* He introduced a method of deep-sea sounding, in which a steel piano wire replaces the ordinary land line. The wire glides so easily to the bottom that 'flying soundings' can be taken while the ship is going at full speed. A pressure gauge to register the depth of the sinker was added by Thomson.

Therefore, *Thomson's marvellous pieces of work have no match as they were unique and have helped man in carrying out their daily chores.* Like many other scientists some of Thomson's predictions were proved false but this great man won a number of honorary degrees for his classic work and is ranked among the famous most scientists of history *as his remarkable work has become the standard texts for many generations of scientists.*